AF469162

North Eastern Railway: sunshine, smoke and steam, as the *Flying Scotsman* leaves Newcastle for Edinburgh around 1900, behind one of the famous class R 4-4-0 locomotives.

A Science Museum Book

The Pre-Grouping Railways

Their development, and individual characters

Part 1

Christine Heap

John van Riemsdijk

London: Her Majesty's Stationery Office

First published 1972
Second impression 1983

ISBN 0 11 290153 0

Contents

List of Illustrations

In colour:

In black and white:

I

II

The colour illustrations are from original oil paintings by F. Moore in the possession of the Science Museum and one of the authors. All except iii are contemporary with the scenes they depict.

I North Eastern Railway Express Train, c. 1913, hauled by three-cylinder 'Atlantic' locomotive of class Z1, designed by Vincent Raven.

II Patrick Stirling's first 'Eight Footer', G.N.R. no. 1 of 1870, alongside Nigel Gresley's second 'Pacific', G.N.R. no. 1471 'Sir Frederick Banbury', built in 1922.

III

IV

V

V On the occasion of a tour by the Prince of Wales, the Taff Vale Railway decorated one of its 4-4-2 tank engines. These, designed by T. Hurry Riches, were the first inside cylinder engines of this very popular type, and appeared in 1888.

III The bright red livery of Wolverton adorns McConnell's large 'Bloomer' express engine of the southern division of the L.N.W.R., 1861. The long firebox was characteristic of this exceptionally powerful class, which surpassed the contemporary products of Crewe.

IV Great Western Railway: The Broad Gauge Express Engine 'Sebastopol' (*above*) shows the final form of the type first introduced by Daniel Gooch in 1847. 'Albion' (*below*) was Churchward's third ten-wheeler, and appeared as a 4-6-0 in 1903. In 1904 this engine was converted to a 4-4-2, and ran in that form for three years while being compared with the French 4-4-2 locomotives.

VI

VII

Foreword

The history of the railways of Great Britain is one of progressive amalgamation. In the first half of the nineteenth century, the small unlinked pioneer systems joined up to form a number of important railways possessing through routes. These enlarged themselves by absorbing lesser lines until they reached a peak of prosperity before 1914. The Great War, and the rise of mechanical road transport, produced problems which could only be resolved by the major reorganisation known as the 'grouping', which resulted in the formation of four main railways. This took effect fifty years ago, and it was decided to commemorate this event in a special exhibition at the Science Museum.

The fiftieth anniversary of the grouping coincided with the twenty-fifth anniversary of nationalisation. It also came at a time when the National Railway Museum at York was being actively planned. For these reasons a new publication was felt to be timely, one dealing with railway history in a way which related to the collection to be displayed at York. This volume is the first part of it.

The Museum is indebted to Professor Jack Simmons of the University of Leicester and to Col. T. M. Simmons of the Science Museum for their help with suggestions and proof reading.

VI Midland Railway no. 2634 was one of the first five Midland Compounds built by S. W. Johnson to the ideas of Walter Smith, of the North Eastern Railway. These first appeared in 1901.

VII The London, Tilbury and Southend Railway decorated its no. 80 for the coronation of King George the Fifth in this elaborate style, which even included a fountain playing in front of the smokebox. The engine was built in 1909, the last and largest version of a brilliant series of 4-4-2T engines with outside cylinders built by the L.T.S.R. from 1880 onwards. The basic livery of this engine is little different from the company's standard style.

Introduction

The grouping of the railways of Great Britain under the provisions of the Railways Act of 1921 took effect on 1 January 1923, though there had been some important amalgamations just before that date. The names of the four group companies, with one exception, were new names, in which the historical and even some of the more precise geographical associations of the names of the smaller companies were lost. The one old name perpetuated was that of the Great Western Railway, a company so individualistic that it could not be joined to either of its obvious rivals, and which at the grouping absorbed, rather than amalgamated with, a large number of small companies with which its tracks were linked.

One of the Great Western's rivals was the London and South Western, which joined with the London, Brighton and South Coast and the jointly managed South Eastern and London, Chatham and Dover Railways, to form the Southern Railway. Another was the majestic London and North Western, the largest of all British railway companies, which suffered what was in the event to be an humiliating amalgamation with the Midland Railway (in spite of having itself absorbed the Lancashire and Yorkshire a year earlier) together with three Scottish companies: the Caledonian, the Glasgow and South Western, and the Highland. This group was called the London, Midland and Scottish Railway, and also included the small North Staffordshire, Furness, and Maryport and Carlisle Railways, to say nothing of two important London area lines which had been taken over somewhat earlier by the L. & N.W.R. and the Midland respectively: the North London, and the London, Tilbury and Southend.

The fourth group company was the London and North Eastern, which was an amalgamation of the Great Northern, the North Eastern, and the North British—two English companies and one Scottish which together operated the 'East Coast Route' and, on it, Britain's most famous train, the *Flying Scotsman*—with the Great Eastern, Great Central and Great North of Scotland. The Great Central had once been the Manchester, Sheffield and Lincolnshire, and had absorbed in 1907 the Lancashire, Derbyshire and East Coast, the name of which was misleadingly optimistic. The North Eastern just managed to take over the long defiant Hull and Barnsley before being itself merged in the L.N.E.R. group, but, more important, it had acquired the Stockton and Darlington in 1863, but had left it with a great deal of its separate character for many years. This particular line is widely regarded as the nucleus of the whole national railway system. When the railway centenary was celebrated in 1925, the event 100 years before which was commemorated was the opening of the Stockton and Darlington.

So a daily contact with much history and geography (and even a little euphony) was lost when all these evocative names were replaced by a few rather dull ones. Because the small companies of the past were closely related to particular industrial areas, flows of trade, growths of population or the development of the widespread holiday habit, it seems valuable to economic, social, and technical historians to summarise the histories of the pre-grouping railways and some of their forerunners. There are books on all of them, some very full and admirably researched. Even so, the task of summarising so much history is still a considerable one, and it is hoped that the present publication will be a useful time-saver for historians and enthusiasts alike.

The reader who is not already a railway enthusiast needs to be told about the special fascination of pre-grouping railways. It is a fascination which could still be felt in travelling on British Railways a year or two ago, and if pre-grouping locomotives and carriages are now not to be seen on the national system, at least many stations and other static things are. A cast-iron notice headed 'Cambrian Railways' was still to be found beside a railway line in regular use, in 1972. More surprisingly, a station clock was reconditioned a few years ago, and the dial repainted with the old initials 'L.T. & S.R.'—a company which disappeared in 1912. Cast-iron awning brackets or seat ends, elegantly incorporating railway company initials, are still quite plentiful and give a sudden and pleasurable reminder of our railway history to a traveller preoccupied with the present.

Each pre-grouping railway company had its own personality, and its own special visual character. The most obviously individual thing was the style of painting of the trains. If locomotives were most commonly green, the shade varied greatly, and so did the style of lining out and the choice of supporting colours. Thus, though the Great Northern and its northerly partner, the North Eastern, both used a sort of grass green, the North Eastern in later years painted footplate edges, tender framing, and other lower parts black, with red lines, while the Great Northern used a deep reddish brown with vermilion lines for the equivalent parts of its locomotives. There were red engines: fire-engine coloured on the Brecon and Merthyr, brownish crimson on the Midland, and Indian red on the Furness. Yellow was once the London, Brighton and South Coast colour, while blue in various shades enriched the Great Eastern, the Caledonian, and the Somerset and Dorset, which, incidentally, was one of the few small railways to preserve its identity at the grouping, because it had been jointly run by the London and South Western and the Midland Railways, which found themselves in different groups in 1923. Another railway to survive in the same way was the Midland and Great Northern Joint, which painted its engines a sort of deep orange.

There was only slightly less variety in the colouring of the carriages. Many railways adopted a two-tone colour scheme for these, with some sort of off white above and brown, green or blue below. The Lancashire and Yorkshire, and the London and South Western, both painted the upper parts buff, which the latter railway lined out in vermilion to give a total effect of (smoked) salmon pink. But many railways favoured the natural look of varnished teak, which varied with age from a light golden shade to quite a deep one. This scheme characterised the coaches of the Great Northern, and those which formed the pool of 'East Coast Joint Stock' used on the *Flying Scotsman* and other expresses. The London and North Eastern adopted it, and nothing looked finer than an L.N.E.R. teak coach freshly varnished, with lettering in gold leaf and a white roof.

The visual character was not only a matter of paint. There was an unmistakable quality about the work of the locomotive designer, which he might take from one railway to another, as the elder Drummond did from the North British to the Caledonian, and then to the London and South Western. Or again, a particular designer might set the style for his successors on the railway, as William Adams did on the Great Eastern, with the result that after he had gone to the L.S.W.R. two railways were building engines in the Adams style. And coaches were scarcely less readily identifiable, because of the subtle differences in the curvature of the roof and of the style of panelling. These things survived many successive repaintings, and dirt and neglect in old age. Right up to the end of steam there were unmistakable North Eastern cabs and Midland chimneys, and one could find an authentic Great Northern suburban train in King's Cross station.

Much of the character of the pre-grouping railways was due to the actual routes rather than the companies. King's Cross was always a station full of Scottish voices, and Paddington full of Welsh. Foreign accents at Victoria have been there for over a century—on the London, Chatham and Dover side especially. Goods traffics have changed their character to some extent, and the miscellaneous goods train, proceeding slowly from station to station and pausing to do a little shunting at most of them, has for the most part lost its traffic to the roads, while new traffics are carried in strange wagons specially built to take 100 tons of oil, or 25 of cement, or 10 of detergent packets, in one container. But enormous trains of coal, and huge wagons full of bricks still traverse what was once the North Eastern Railway, and the Western Region still brings milk and early flowers, as well as South Wales coal, to the Metropolis.

It is a commonplace to point out that the building of the railways transformed the world, but the details are seldom specified, though the transformation was the cumulative effect of innumerable detailed changes. The greater part of the British railway system was built in the forty years from 1830 to 1870, and the mere building of the lines required an annual consumption of iron well in excess of the total national output before the work started. From about 1870, steel rails replaced the iron ones. This meant that first the iron industry, then the steel industry, had to develop rapidly simply to cope with railway expansion. The same could be said of the timber trade, the brick industry, and all aspects of civil engineering. Equally obvious is the importance of the railways to the mechanical engineering industry, which, in the early years, provided all the locomotives and carriages, and remained an important provider of these things after the individual railway companies built their own workshops.

Scientific technology benefited greatly, too. The Great Western installed the first railway telegraph system between Paddington and Slough in 1842, and this was the first real use of the electric telegraph for a serious purpose—the regulation of traffic on a railway line. Once installed, it found other uses, such as the celebrated tracking down of the murderer Tawell, which captured the imagination of the public and led to the use of the system for private messages. And so a national telegraph and later, telephone system evolved, many of its wires running along the familiar telegraph poles beside the tracks, which provided a wayleave ready for the purpose.

Each of the old companies was called into existence to serve some real or imagined local or regional need, but soon developed a will of its own, sending out branch lines to tap traffic as a plant sends out roots to find water. Rivalry with adjoining companies sometimes led to open warfare, in which locomotives were imprisoned and heads broken, as happened when the London and South Western and the London, Brighton and South Coast fought over Portsmouth. A more peaceful and profitable rivalry was romantically expressed by the great train races to Edinburgh in 1888 and to Aberdeen in 1895, in which the East Coast and West Coast alliances of companies fought night after night to cut the times of their journeys until a truce was called, and an agreement reached between the two sides in the interests of safety no less than of economics. Meanwhile, the third rival, the Midland Railway, with a longer and more severely graded route, joined with the Glasgow and South Western in providing a higher standard of comfort for third-class passengers than either of its great rivals, and thereby made its contribution to the improvement of travel by train.

Railways were often shipping companies and dock owners too. The Great Western was engaged in the Irish traffic, as were the L.N.W.R., the L.Y.R., the Midland, and the Glasgow and South Western. G.W.R. and L.S.W.R. both served the Channel Islands, while mainland Europe was the destination of many passengers using the L.S.W.R., the L.B.S.C.R., and the S.E.C.R. to the south of London, and the Great Eastern, the Great Northern and North Eastern lines to east coast ports. Even the little London, Tilbury and Southend had its boat expresses, mainly for ocean liners, but a few for services to Holland and Belgium. Perhaps the greatest coup in this field was achieved by the L.S.W.R. which took over Southampton Docks and so developed them as to take most of the transatlantic traffic away from the mighty L.N.W.R. and Liverpool.

The encouragement of suburban growth was the speciality of the companies which eventually formed the Southern group. With no rich industrial area to serve and only a seasonal holiday traffic to fill their long-distance trains, they pursued policies the effects of which can be seen today in the suburbanisation of virtually all of Surrey, and much of Kent, Sussex and Hampshire. The Great Eastern did the same for a large corner of Essex. By way of contrast, the Great Northern was reluctant to stop anywhere south of the East Midlands, served the towns of St. Albans and Hertford only at the end of single track branch lines, and seriously considered closing down its suburban station at Finsbury Park as a result of every shareholders' meeting in the earlier years of the company's existence. The G.N.R. and the Midland never attached much importance to suburban traffic, though they were obliged to take some notice of the spread of the capital, and the G.N.R. did adopt some locally sponsored lines. But to this day, London ends much more abruptly on its northern side than it does to the South, East, or West.

The grouping was inevitable. There were so many rival routes unable to co-exist economically even before the days of mechanical road transport, and so much unprofitable competition between routes otherwise sufficiently well provided with traffic to pay their way. Rivalry did not end with the grouping, but irrational rivalry did. All the same, there was much loss. With sixteen principal railway companies, as against the post-grouping four, there was great scope for individual experiment, without which progress could hardly have been made as rapidly as it was. There were also excellent career prospects for men of talent, who could achieve high responsibility young, and move from company to company, gaining expertise, comparing conditions, and providing original thinking at a level where it could be put into practice.

With the present level of scientific knowledge we can perhaps dispense with a variety of approaches to the problems of our railways, and the uniform blue livery on our trains is an apt symbol of the modern railway. But the enthusiast will be forgiven for dreaming of Carlisle Citadel in pre-grouping days, with six major railways sending in their trains behind locomotives of six totally different colours; bright green for the North Eastern, black for the North Western, brown for the North British, blue for the Caledonian, dark green with red for the Glasgow and South Western, and crimson on the engines of the old Midland Railway.

MAJOR ROUTES OF THE NORTH EASTERN RAILWAY

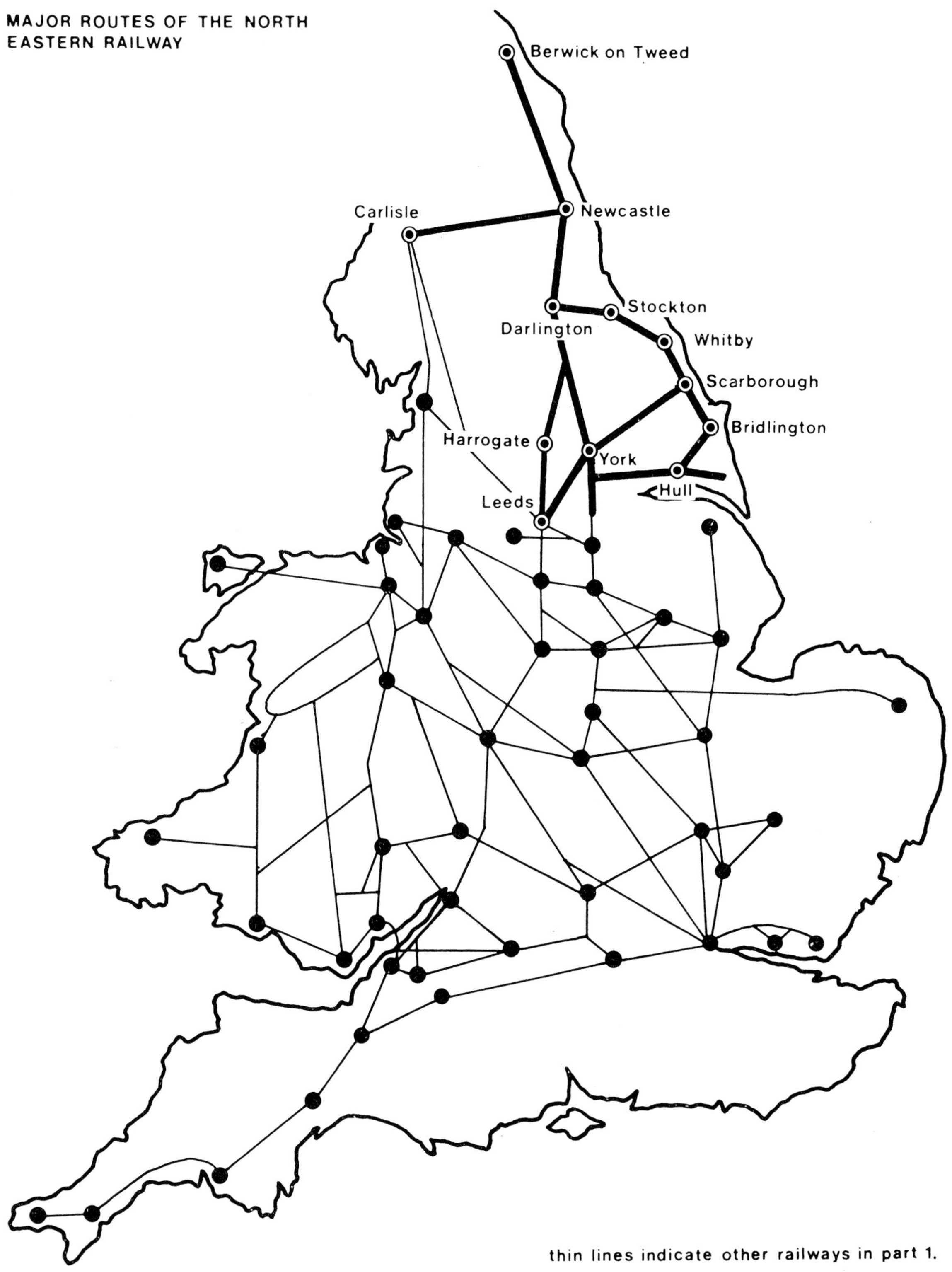

thin lines indicate other railways in part 1.

The North Eastern Railway

1 A contemporary sketch of the opening of the Stockton and Darlington Railway in 1825. The name on the carriage is a later addition.

Of all the pre-grouping railways, the North Eastern could claim seniority. It incorporated within its large and complex system of lines the historic Stockton and Darlington Railway, opened in 1825 and absorbed within the N.E.R. in 1863. 1825 is the date from which the railway system, as distinct from a few unconnected private industrial lines, began to develop, and the Stockton and Darlington was also the first public railway to use steam locomotives. Its opening was a great local occasion, with a far greater world significance, and George Stephenson, civil and mechanical engineer to the line, drove his little engine *Locomotion* into immortality, and made his own name the most famous in the history of engineering.

Locomotion is preserved on Darlington station, now an important stop on the 'East Coast Route' from King's Cross to Edinburgh and Aberdeen, for the North Eastern was a railway with a strong sense of history. Its lines monopolised the area in which railways began, the area around George Stephenson's birthplace at Wylam on Tyne, and the scene of Hedley's experiments on the adhesion of a smooth wheel upon a smooth rail which led to the building of *Puffing Billy*. Nearby was Killingworth, where Stephenson himself built his early engines, and the Hetton Colliery where one now preserved in York Railway Museum was also used.

The Stockton and Darlington was absorbed, but not smothered, by the North Eastern. For a number of years it functioned almost as an independent railway, and its works, originally at Shildon but from just before the North Eastern takeover sited at Darlington, eventually became the main locomotive building works of the larger company. Material preserved by the North Eastern also formed the basis of the first railway museum in the country at York.

It was only to be expected that a railway with such beginnings, and in such a predominantly industrial area, should be in the forefront of railway engineering, and it had some spectacular bridges and viaducts, the extraordinary two-level structure at Newcastle being perhaps the best known. But it was undoubtedly the locomotives which were most distinctively North Eastern.

In the early days Edward Fletcher presided over the works at Gateshead, while Thomas Bouch looked after the Stockton and Darlington section at Shildon and later at Darlington. Bouch built locomotives to the Stephenson 'long boiler' pattern for the predominantly mineral traffic of his line, and one of these, built in 1874, survived the grouping and was preserved to take part in the railway centenary celebrations of 1925, after which it retired to York Railway Museum where it now arouses astonishment at the loving elaboration of the paintwork bestowed upon a humble mineral engine a century ago.

Fletcher was one of those patient engineers who adopted a basic concept of the locomotive and then slowly eliminated every possible source of trouble. He also cared for the external appearance and favoured elegantly curving cabs, shining brass, and complicated colour schemes based on the bright green which was to remain the North Eastern colour even after the grouping. One of his 901 class is also at York and it is worth recalling that the locomotive crews were so appreciative of Fletcher that when his successor attempted to make some small alterations to these locomotives there was so acute a reaction that the unfortunate man, Alexander McDonnell, had eventually to resign. Fletcher had always listened to the comments of the locomotive crews, and his engines not only did their work well, but were comfortable for the men to handle. Many of them lasted well into the days of the L.N.E.R.

After the McDonnell fiasco, a committee under Henry Tennant, the general manager, immediately prepared designs for an enlarged version of Fletcher's 901 class 2-4-0. The footplatemen took to these engines with enthusiasm and during the race to Edinburgh in 1888 they drove them frequently at 75 miles per hour. One of these is also preserved at York, as is a 4-4-0 of Wilson Worsdell's M class which did some notable racing in the 1895 races to Aberdeen.

The successor eventually appointed to Fletcher's office was Wilson Worsdell's elder brother, Thomas. This was perhaps an injustice to the younger man, who had had a large share in designing the 'Tennant' engines, but Thomas Worsdell had held the job of locomotive superintendent with the Great Eastern Railway, where

2 Thomas Worsdell's large compound single driver locomotive of class J: probably the most powerful and fastest express engine of its time, 1889.

he had been able to study the work of the great William Adams, and had created a number of standard types which were to be perpetuated with minor modifications for many years. Some of these, such as the 2-4-2 tanks, he brought to the North Eastern. However, he had also experimented with compounding and this he developed very greatly in his new position. The Worsdell-von Borries compounds had two cylinders, inside, and he built them for every kind of service. Most unusually, he even built fifty 0-6-2 tank engines with this arrangement. Among his compounds was one really outstanding class, the large class J 4-2-2 express engine of 1889. One of these under test put out more than a thousand horsepower, at 86 miles per hour, with a 300-ton train—a performance which made it by some margin the most powerful express engine of its day, and possibly also the fastest. Even by today's standards, the power to weight ratio of this class was extremely good.

Thomas Worsdell retired owing to ill health at the early age of 53, and his brother, who succeeded him, eventually converted all his engines, with one exception, to simple expansion. Undoubtedly, the valve gearing of the compounds was a source of trouble, and the celebrated difficulties of F. W. Webb on the London and North Western (with compounds of greatly inferior design) did not encourage Wilson Worsdell, so a brilliant beginning came in the end to nothing. The one compound survivor was the little tank engine *Aerolite*, a much rebuilt machine used for hauling light inspection trains, and this sole survivor of a once numerous and highly promising type of locomotive is fittingly in York Railway Museum.

Thomas Worsdell's locomotives, rebuilt as simples, lasted long, some of them into the 1960s (as did some of his Great Eastern ones). His special legacy to the North Eastern was the beautiful cab with two windows in each side, solidly built and wood lined. It was as comfortable as elegant, and although other railways eventually began to provide something similar, the Worsdell cab remained unsurpassed. It epitomised the concern and respect shown by the N.E.R. for the men who carried the high responsibility of working their trains. It also contributed largely to the elegance and the air of prosperity which marked the North Eastern locomotives, and hence, the railway itself.

Wilson Worsdell produced the M class already mentioned in 1892. Looking at 1621 as she stands in York Railway Museum it is hard to realise that this light and elegant machine was once the heaviest express engine in the country, and belonged to a class known as 'rail crushers'. Built as simples, these engines were planned to be easily converted to compound working, and one of them was actually built as such. This engine, 1619, was mainly due to Walter Smith, Worsdell's brilliant chief draughtsman. He was responsible for her rebuilding into a three-cylinder compound, in 1898, in which form she served as the prototype for the celebrated compounds of the Midland Railway, of which eventually there were 240, the last being built by the L.M.S. in 1932. The explanation of this adoption of what was essentially Smith's design by the Midland lies in the long-standing friendship between Smith and S. W. Johnson of the Midland. The first of the Midland engines is also preserved in the York Railway Museum.

Smith was probably the main influence in the design of the class R 4-4-0, which were an outstanding success and had a life of half a century on passenger work. His distinctive touch was seen in the use of a high boiler pressure for the day—200 lbs. per sq. inch was the sort of pressure used only for compounds in 1899, but the R class were simples—and in the use of piston valves, of which Smith was at this time the only really successful exponent. Unfortunately, Smith, like Worsdell senior, suffered ill-health, and although he did produce two very fine compound 4-4-2 express engines, he did not live to see just how good they were. With his death, the cause of compounding in Britain lost its only really successful advocate.

In place of compounding, three cylinder simple propulsion became the North Eastern practice for the most powerful types. It was first applied by Wilson Worsdell to some heavy tank engines for shunting, but his successor, Sir Vincent Raven applied it to many other types, and most notably to his large 'Atlantics' of class Z and Z1, later versions of some two-cylinder 'Atlantics' designed by Worsdell. These 'Atlantic' or 4-4-2 engines were a feature of the East Coast Route from very early in the twentieth century until the last war. The Great Northern had first introduced the type in 1898, and the North British eventually did so too, though the G.N. and N.B. types were very different from the N.E.R. ones, which were the largest and heaviest of the type.

All these engines looked magnificent, and the goods engines which predominated all over the system looked scarcely less so, for though the style of painting was in later years a red-lined black, the standard of finish and design was in no way inferior. North Eastern engines were always amply powerful for their work and quiet in operation. They gave the impression of supreme competence. And in fact the last big engines of the pre-grouping era to remain in service on British Railways were North Eastern eight-coupled goods engines which lasted till the end of steam.

The carriages on the system matched the locomotives. The older engines were usually coupled to equally elegant coaches of David Bain's design, with high clerestories on their roofs, while the newer and more massive machines hauled large modern coaches of wine-coloured stock, or the beautiful golden teak-finished vehicles of the East Coast Joint Stock, mostly of a design based on the practice of the Great Northern, with high elliptical roofs the ends of which turned down to meet the rounded ends of the carriages. There were low clerestories on some of these, and many ran on twelve wheels, which was an expensive but effective way of eliminating the feel of the rail joints, also practised on the west coast route.

These splendid trains, and the long trains of coal, iron ore, steel or bricks, ran through some very fine stations with high arched roofs, of which those at Newcastle, Darlington and York are the best known survivors. York is probably the finest of all, the long vaulted roofs being set on the curve of the platforms, and carrying the eye forward in a long movement to where the tracks swing out of sight—a tantalising invitation to travel.

Because the North Eastern's rail network, for the major part of its route mileage, lay in the industrial mining areas of Durham and Yorkshire (though its main line stretched on through Northumberland to the Scottish border) the story of its development is largely that of the local lines built to link the mining and industrial towns of the region with the rivers and the sea.

For our purposes it begins with the Stockton and Darlington line engineered by George Stephenson and, excluding its short branch lines to various collieries along the way, twenty-six and a quarter miles in length. In common with the earlier wagon ways of the industrial areas, the Stockton and Darlington line was built primarily to carry coal, bricks and other goods, in this case to the Tees estuary, but the Act of Parliament authorising its construction had also permitted the transportation of passengers, something rather rare although not new at this time. Its success established a new form of transport, the public steam railway, and led before long to the opening of the Canterbury and Whitstable and Liverpool and Manchester railways, the latter being the first important main line, opened in 1830.

In Durham many lines were built, running to and from the mines. In 1828 the Clarence Railway obtained its Act for a line from Haverton Hill on the Tees to Simpasture on the Stockton and Darlington Railway. In 1834 the Stanhope and Tyne Railway was opened to South Shields, and the Durham and Sunderland Railway obtained permission for a line via Moorsley and Ryhope, to Sunderland. While old collieries remained unserved and new collieries were opened in Durham, new lines continued to be built, until a complex system of local railways had been created in the district.

In Yorkshire, the Leeds and Selby Railway, connecting with the river Ouse, was opened in 1834 and extended from Selby to Hull in 1840. Access to Whitby, then an aspiring East Yorkshire port, was assured with the opening of a line from Pickering in 1836. The previous year had seen the formation of the famous York and North Midland Railway Company, with George Hudson, the Railway King, as its chairman. The company's first undertaking was to build a line from York to Normanton to connect with the North Midland line from Derby and give a through route from London to York. In 1844 the same company obtained permission to build a line from York to Scarborough with a branch from Malton to join the Whitby and Pickering line, and in 1845 it began work on lines from Scarborough to Bridlington and from Bridlington to Hull, via Beverley and Driffield.

3 Newcastle from the South West, in 1849.

The Leeds and Thirsk Railway also obtained its Act in 1845, for the line which it was eventually to extend to Stockton on Tees.

As early as 1835 it had been proposed to build a line from York to Newcastle, to continue the north-south rail link, and by 1841 the first stretch of this line from York to Darlington had been completed. Three years later came the Darlington to Newcastle section and finally in 1847 when the line through Morpeth and Alnmouth was opened, Newcastle was linked with Berwick.

Such had been the pattern of railway development in this part of the country, when the North Eastern Railway Company was formed in 1854. The York, Newcastle and Berwick Railway, the York and North Midland, the Leeds Northern (which had originally been the Leeds and Thirsk) and the Malton and Driffield were the original constituent members of the N.E.R. They were joined in 1862, by the Newcastle and Carlisle Railway and in 1863, by the Stockton and Darlington.

The North Eastern's main northern line began originally at Knottingley and ran through York, Northallerton, Darlington, Durham, Newcastle and on to Berwick, where connection was made with the North British Railway Company serving Edinburgh, Glasgow, Dundee and Aberdeen. To left and right of this main trunk route, North Eastern lines ran from Leeds to Harrogate, Northallerton and Stockton; from Leeds to Selby and Hull; from York to Scarborough and Whitby; from Darlington to Stockton and Hartlepool and from Newcastle to Carlisle and Sunderland.

The North Eastern was from its beginning the only major railway company in this rich mining and trading area of England and by a policy of continued absorption of smaller lines, it was to maintain its virtual monopoly to the end. There were of course, several attempts by other independent companies to encroach on North Eastern territory, but they usually failed through lack of finance and either faded out of their own accord or were taken over by the N.E.R., before they had time to become established in the region.

Such at least had been the pattern until 1880, when the Hull and Barnsley Railway obtained its Act. This valiant company, through numerous financial and other difficulties, managed to remain independent and to tap the North Eastern's Hull traffic until just before the 1923 railway grouping, when it finally succumbed to its larger neighbour.

Goods traffic greatly overshadowed the passenger traffic. The North Eastern, in fact, carried more mineral and other goods, and with the exception of the Midland, had more wagon rolling-stock than any other contemporary British railway company. Coal was the preponderant mineral on the line, being shipped from several ports within the compass of the N.E.R. The Tyne docks, the Blyth and Dunston docks, the docks at Hartlepool, Sunderland and Hull were all important in this respect. The Tyne, the Hartlepool and the Hull docks also dealt with considerable amounts of timber. The Middlesbrough docks on the Stockton and Darlington extension line were actually owned by the North Eastern Railway, and in 1874 the company undertook to increase the docking area from 6 to 12 acres, and to widen the entrance for larger ocean-going ships, so that the Cleveland iron trade, which had grown steadily since 1852, could be economically exploited.

Similar improvements, for the benefit of the fishing trade this time, were begun at

4 Corridor non-vestibuled third-class coach, N.E.R., *c*. 1910.

5 The North Eastern was a pioneer of local electric services. This is one of the original trains used on the North Tyne branches, in 1914.

Hull in 1893, when, under the General Managership of George S. Gibb, the N.E.R. finally took over those docks which had belonged to the Hull Dock Company. In fact Gibb, during his period in office (1891–1906), did much both for N.E.R. freight and passenger services by reorganising their administration, dividing responsibility for the handling and moving of traffic between separate operating and commercial sections, and increasing the average load of goods trains by as much as 50%.

The North Eastern Railway, besides handling its great volume of goods traffic, also formed a vital link in the East Coast London-Scottish passenger service, and during the chairmanship of H. S. Thompson (1855-74) several improvements were made to this main northern line. The most important of these improvements was probably the 1870 extension of the North Eastern track, from York, via Selby, to make an end-on junction with the Great Northern Railway, just outside Doncaster. This afforded a more direct East Coast route from London to Scotland and dispensed with the necessity of sending trains over the Lancashire and Yorkshire line from Doncaster to Knottingley.

1872 saw the completion of a line through the Team valley, to shorten the main line route from Darlington to Newcastle, and in 1877, the impressive new passenger station at York was opened. Built outside the city walls, the station was organised in such a way as to permit through running of East Coast trains which had previously needed to reverse before continuing their journey.

The North Eastern, of course, worked closely with the Great Northern and the

North British in running this Anglo-Scottish service, and from 1868 most of the rolling-stock used on the route was in fact owned jointly by the G.N., the N.B. and the N.E. railways. The 'East Coast Joint Stock', as it was called, had to be of a high standard to compete with that of the parallel West Coast service, and much progress in external design and internal comfort resulted from the rivalry of the two routes. The East Coast companies had one triumph in introducing the first sleeping-cars to be used on the Scottish run in 1873, nearly one year before similar cars were used on the West Coast route. The East Coast companies were also first to begin construction of corridor carriages in this country, but unfortunately from their point of view, not the first to put them into service. Similarly, third-class dining cars, although first conceived by the East Coast group in 1891, were in service on the West Coast route just a few weeks before they appeared on the East. Rumours of the East Coast's plans had early reached the West, and the carriage building firm responsible for the work had been unable to honour the original delivery date of the East Coast stock. But in spite of these disappointments in the fight to be first, the East Coast Joint Stock was comfortable and well turned out, and finished handsomely in varnished teak. In 1900, the most luxurious of the ECJ trains were produced in two sets of 65 ft., 12-wheeled carriages, with Pullman vestibules, built for the famous *Flying Scotsman*. These were to become the standard ECJ coaches and were to rival the L.N.W. 12-wheelers for ease and comfort in riding.

The London-Scottish passenger service was only a fraction of the North Eastern's passenger traffic. Besides running daily services from the larger towns within its area to the popular coastal resorts such as Bridlington, Scarborough, Whitby and Robin Hood's Bay, N.E. passenger trains reached much further afield. 1883 saw the first N.E. express service from Newcastle to Liverpool, and with the opening of the new Great Central spur from Woodford to join the Great Western Railway at Banbury, the North Eastern began operating an express from Newcastle to Bournemouth, travelling via Leicester and Banbury. From 1905, the company began operating its own steamers to the Continent and from 1907, in conjunction with the Lancashire and Yorkshire Railway, ran a tri-weekly passenger and freight service from Hull to Belgium and back.

The N.E.R. had an enterprising approach to excursion traffic and campaigned vigorously for the east coast resorts which it served. At one time books of coupons for cut-price travel were on sale, each allowing 1000 miles by train. As early as 1860, the North Eastern had begun a policy of reductions in first- and second-class fares to stimulate greater use of its services, and had abolished the supplementary charge for travel in express trains, once a common feature of railway fare structure, in 1861.

At the beginning of the twentieth century the N.E.R. attempted with some success to create a pattern of commuter traffic, by persuading the businessmen of the West Riding to settle in the resorts of Bridlington, Filey, and fashionable Scarborough. They offered journey times of just under 1½ hours, which represented some brisk running. Not all N.E.R. trains were fast, because the company had a virtual monopoly in most of the area it served, but for a number of years it ran the fastest train in Great Britain, which covered the 44½ miles from Darlington to York in 43 minutes.

By 1914, the North Eastern had reached the peak of its development and was one of the most successful and highly regarded of the pre-grouping railway companies. From the early years, when the different companies it had taken over had retained their own individuality, their own workshops, their own designers and independent styles of working, the N.E.R. had become a unified concern. The hub of the system was York, where the N.E.R. played host to seven other companies in its magnificent station—a sufficient indication of the crucial position of this railway in the nation's economy. And under that vast and curving roof, the splendidly architectural North Eastern locomotives, their spacious, windowed cabs lined with polished wood and their bright green boilers adorned with polished brasswork, wore an unmistakable air of prosperity.

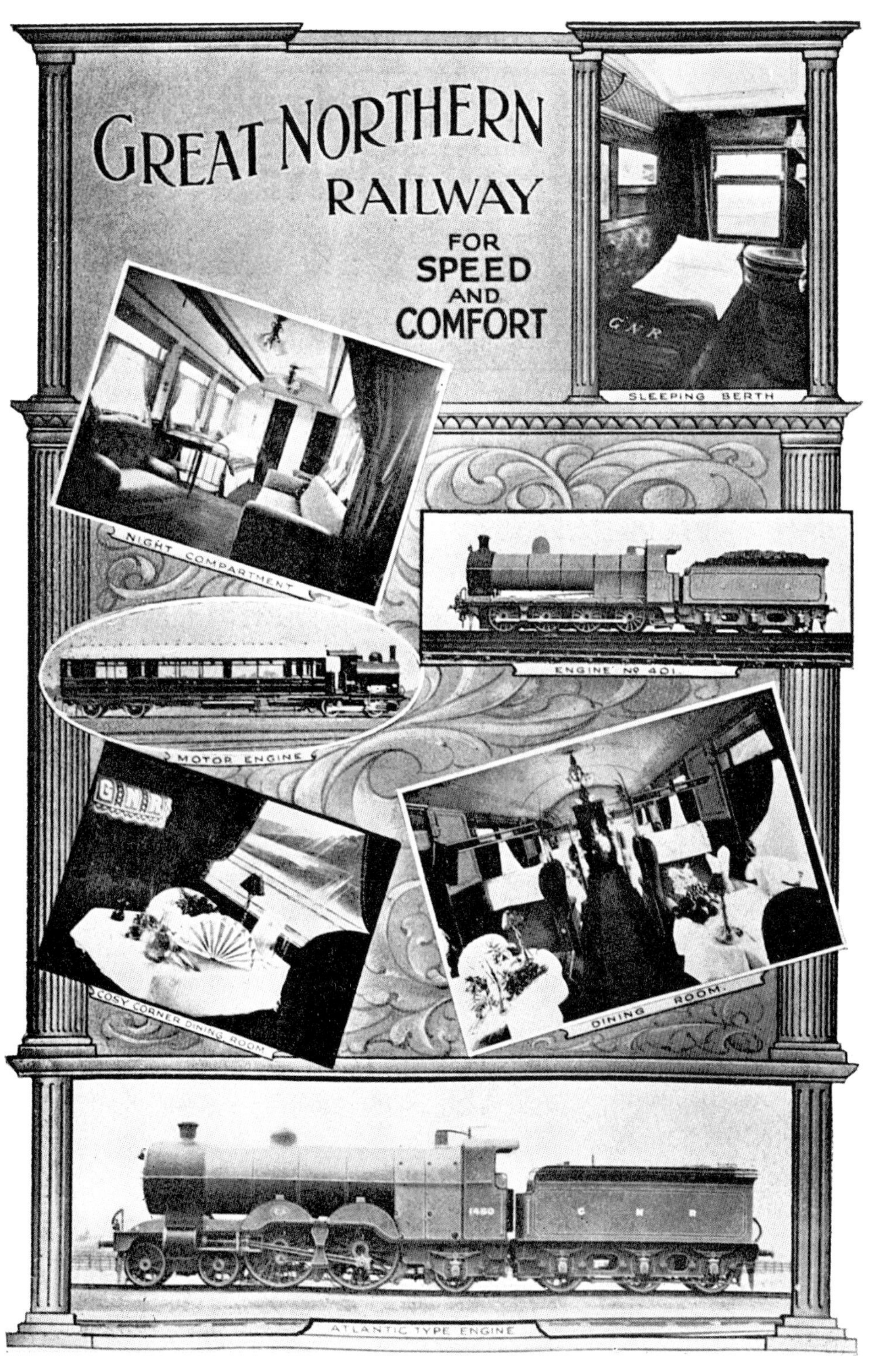
GREAT NORTHERN
RAILWAY
FOR
SPEED
AND
COMFORT
SLEEPING BERTH
NIGHT COMPARTMENT
ENGINE Nº 401.
MOTOR ENGINE
COSY CORNER DINING ROOM
DINING ROOM.
ATLANTIC TYPE ENGINE

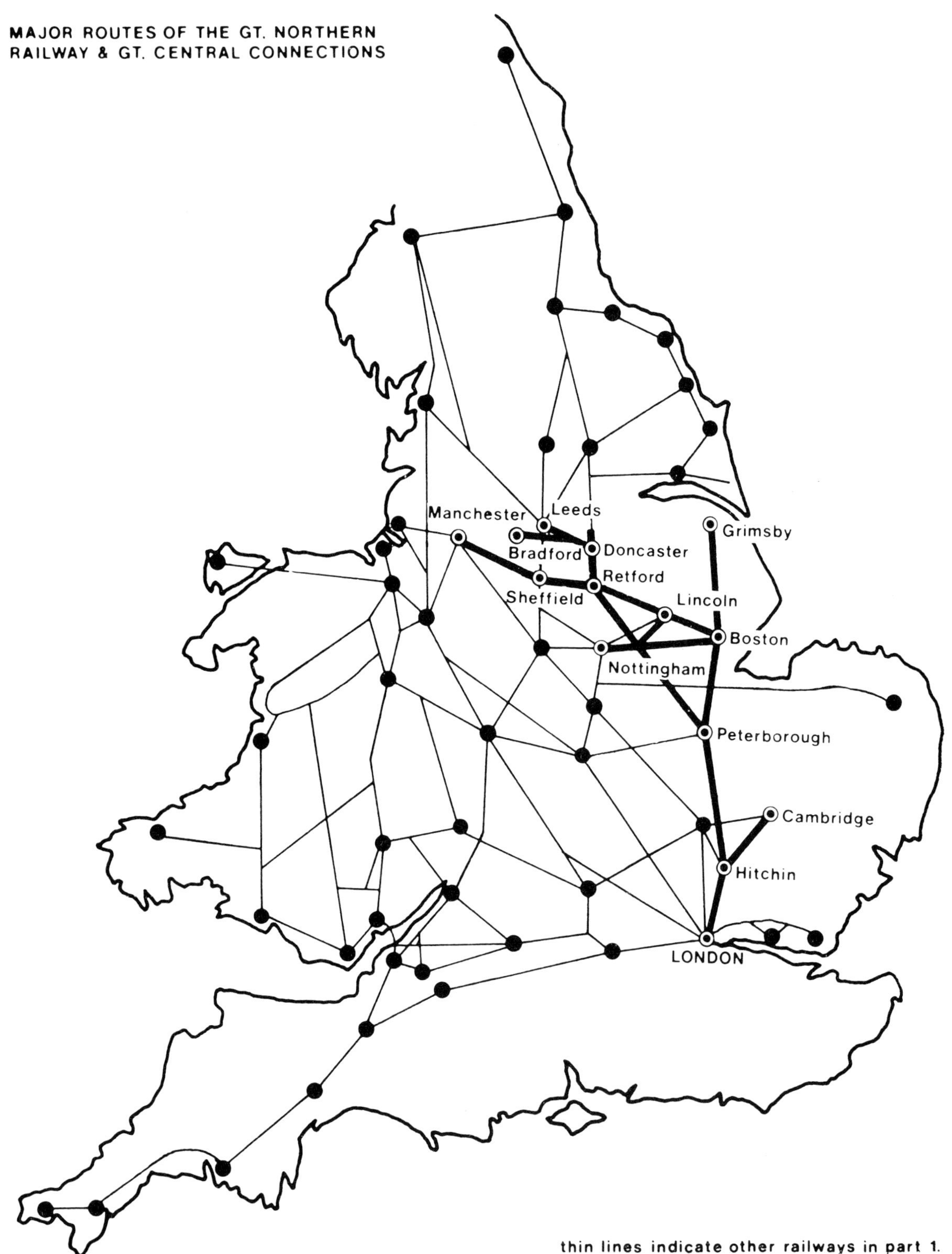
MAJOR ROUTES OF THE GT. NORTHERN
RAILWAY & GT. CENTRAL CONNECTIONS
Manchester
Leeds
Bradford
Doncaster
Grimsby
Retford
Sheffield
Lincoln
Boston
Nottingham
Peterborough
Cambridge
Hitchin
LONDON
thin lines indicate other railways in part 1.

The Great Northern Railway

The pre-grouping railways bequeathed fourteen London terminal stations to posterity, to count only those carrying main line traffic, and they are all still in use. Generally, the greater the distance the trains travelled, the more grandiose the terminus. The colossal arch and flanking pavilions of Euston were not actually designed with the Inverness trains in mind, for these did not yet exist, but they certainly provided the boldest assertion of a railway's importance, at least until work started on the new station at Milan in the 1920s. In the case of Euston pride came before a fall, and the effect of what now stands where that Doric portico once stood is entirely different, and perhaps a good deal more inviting.

By way of contrast, King's Cross, the London terminus of the Great Northern Railway, proclaims itself to be no more than a simple train shed, with a double barrel-vault roof. Though reputedly modelled on some stables of the Tsar, it seems to have been planned as a good place to contain trains and shelter their passengers, and its simple facade pretends to no other function. St. Pancras has a finer roof, of later construction, but this is hidden from the road by another architectural declaration of importance in the shape of a hotel—a hotel which is actually in the shape of something else, romantic, ecclesiastical, and hard to define.

St. Pancras towers above King's Cross, being built upon an enormous beer cellar provided for the trade from Burton. Perhaps also it expresses an unjustified sense of superiority, for the Midland Railway which built it had long had a sense of grievance against the Great Northern, though it had gained access for its own trains to the capital via G.N.R. metals from Hitchin, before it erected St. Pancras.

These three great stations still symbolise the struggles of over a century ago, when the idea of what became the G.N.R.—the idea of a straight route from London to York, and so via the N.E.R. to Scotland—aroused the most violent hostility of George Hudson, the unspeakable 'Railway King'. Hudson ruled the Midland Railway, which at that time connected to London via Rugby and Euston. In spite of every conceivable unscrupulous attempt, Hudson could not stop the G.N.R. getting its Act of Parliament, but even when the line was built, King's Cross opened (in 1852), and Hudson in disgrace for his financial manipulations, Euston was still the headquarters of a protracted conspiracy against the newcomer, directed by Mark Huish of the mighty London and North Western Railway.

However, King's Cross, lying low in what at first was a disreputable part of London, provided the fastest trains, and to many destinations had the shorter route. The Great Northern was in some ways a very unpretentious railway, and King's Cross set the style of the whole line. None of its stations was anything but plain, though not in the sense of ugly. The carriages were plain varnished teak, though as the years went by the roofs became white, and more gold appeared on the sides, making eventually an extremely handsome livery yet one which still showed

7 Patrick Stirling's elegant eight-foot single in its earlier form, as built from 1870.

clearly that the carriages were made of wood, just as the facade of King's Cross showed that it was the front of a train shed. The locomotives never sported much brasswork, and in the later years of the railway's independent existence only three of them bore names.

The engineering was superb. The line itself, after an initial steep climb up through tunnels from the terminal's low situation, swept northward with few curves and over gradients which presented small difficulty except to the heaviest trains. Track and structures were solid, and there were seven tunnels in the first 15 miles of the main line, as the rails cut through the ridges of high ground on the way out of the Thames valley. At Digswell a long plain brick viaduct, 100 ft. high, massive and dead straight, carries the railway across the wide green valley of the insignificant Mimram, taking trains ten times as heavy and twice as fast as the ones it was built for.

William Cubitt was engineer of the line. The locomotive engineers were an illustrious four named Archibald Sturrock, Patrick Stirling, Henry Ivatt and Nigel Gresley, and all four in their different periods were right in the forefront of technical progress. Great Northern trains were always among the fastest, and also among the heaviest. Towards the end of the nineteenth century the G.N.R. perhaps indulged its preference for six-wheeled carriages a little too long, but when the change came most of the expresses were well provided with carriages having twelve, a luxury made unnecessary nowadays by the use of long welded rails, but all too seldom provided in the days of noticeable rail joints.

The long periods in office of the locomotive engineers are worth noting. Stirling had 30 years, and so did Gresley, though 18 years of his time were spent as locomotive engineer of the L.N.E.R. Ivatt had 15. Stirling set the locomotive style of the company, in a great number of small but austerely elegant locomotives, and one rather larger class of unusual beauty, the eight-foot 'single drivers' with outside cylinders and their huge wheels largely exposed in a decidedly unVictorian manner. They were perhaps the most celebrated and admired locomotives of their day, and performed with remarkable excellence and reliability. During the railway races to the

8 The first British Atlantic, and the first true express engine in the country to have ten wheels, Ivatt's no. 990, later named *Henry Oakley*. Because the type appeared in 1898, they were always known as 'Klondykes'.

North in 1888 and 1895, these engines never failed to achieve the timings required of them by the Superintendent of the Line, Francis Cockshott, who for many years saw to it that the G.N.R. ran faster than all its rivals.

Henry Ivatt was the first British engineer to produce a ten-wheeled express engine, and one of the very few to make such engines really superior to eight-wheeled types around the turn of the century. He succeeded by taking the Stirling 'Eight Footer' as the basis of his new design, and producing a 4-4-2 in place of a 4-2-2. In 1898, 28 years after the first 'eight footer' was built, he built no. 990, later named *Henry Oakley* after the general manager. He followed this up in 1902 with his large 'Atlantic'—the same engine chassis with an enormous boiler upon it, having, for the first time in Britain, a wide firebox spreading over the trailing wheels. These engines became as famous as the eight footers, and in a long life which ended just at the time of nationalisation, they maintained the G.N.R. tradition of high speed, capable of exceeding 90 miles per hour, and the haulage of very heavy trains. One of them, no longer new, was once observed to take a 17-coach express from Grantham to York at an average of nearly 70 miles per hour for much of the way. The first Stirling 'eight footer', no. 1 ; *Henry Oakley* and the first of Ivatt's large 'Atlantics', no. 251, are all happily preserved in the Railway Museum at York.

It was after the grouping that Gresley earned his reputation, and his knighthood, as the engineer of very high-speed trains. He succeeded Ivatt not long before the first world war and the first Gresley design was a 2-6-0 for mixed traffic, including the fish trains from North Sea ports which were a feature of the G.N.R. But in 1922 he built his first 4-6-2 *Great Northern*, the forerunner of that long and famous series of locomotives of which the third was *Flying Scotsman* and which later were built streamlined.

The Great Northern was the southern partner of the North Eastern in the East Coast route. It was a smaller concern, and its style was very different, yet in the end

9 Nigel Gresley's first new design for the G.N.R.: his first 'Mogul' or 2-6-0 mixed traffic locomotive of 1913.

its style dominated the Anglo-Scottish expresses, even before the grouping. This was perhaps because most of the pressure for faster schedules on those services came from the G.N.R., especially from Cockshott at the time of the races. But then the railway had been conceived specifically to shorten the time and distance between Yorkshire and London, so the role of pacemaker was a natural one for it to play in the partnership.

The Act of Parliament of 1846 finally authorising the formation of the Great Northern Railway Company combined two previously conflicting plans for a new route north to Doncaster and York: the one proposing a line from London through Peterborough, Lincoln and Gainsborough; the other proposing a more direct line from London, through Peterborough, Grantham and Retford.

This latter proposal seemed to present a serious threat to the Midland Railway's existing northern route which meandered over London and Birmingham metals from London, and passed through Rugby and Derby before turning into Sheffield and on towards York—hence the hostility of Hudson.

Confusion over the exact route for the direct line, bad weather conditions and failing finances delayed and finally altered the plans of the new company. Work began at once, not on the main line but on the loop line from Peterborough as far as Lincoln, with a branch running from Boston to Grimsby. Not until 1867 was the loop line completed from Lincoln to Doncaster via Gainsborough and until then, the G.N. sent its trains into Doncaster over the metals of the Manchester, Sheffield and Lincolnshire Railway, via Retford.

Shortage of funds held up construction of the Peterborough to London line but in 1850 this section of the G.N. system, with a temporary London terminus at Maiden Lane, was opened throughout. The Retford to Doncaster and Askern Junction stretch of the main line was under construction by 1848, but the middle section of track linking Peterborough and Retford was slow in coming, partly because of heavy rain in 1851. As a result, the completed direct northern line from London, as far as Askern Junction, was not finally opened until August 1852. The new Great Northern London station at King's Cross was completed and opened some weeks later.

Askern Junction was as far north as the Great Northern track penetrated. Plans for the line to York had been abandoned and G.N. trains going north of Askern

Junction ran over Lancashire and Yorkshire metals to Knottingley where they transferred to the York and North Midland line (later a part of the North Eastern company).

Even while still engaged in laying its track the Great Northern had been faced by more serious difficulties. A line from London, linking eventually with the North Eastern's line through York to Berwick, provided an East Coast route to Scotland, parallel to that of the L.N.W.R., and Mark Huish, general manager of the North Western, was aware of the fact. In 1850, therefore, he had formed the 'Euston Square Confederacy' to which the L.N.W., the Midland, the Lancashire and Yorkshire, the Manchester, Sheffield and Lincolnshire, and the Edinburgh and Glasgow Railways, all at one time or another belonged. Their plan was simply to arrange traffic whenever possible to the disadvantage of the Great Northern. For seven years this confederacy operated, to some extent successfully, but at the end of it all, with the guidance and determination of Edmund Denison, its chairman, and Seymour Clarke, its general manager, the G.N. still survived, and indeed under this pressure had been forced to offer improved services and seek its own agreements with rival companies.

Opening later than most other railways in Britain, the Great Northern always used rolling-stock of a reasonably high standard. All its third-class carriages were enclosed and fitted with wooden bench seats, while its second-class coaches even had cushions. In an early attempt to attract passengers to the Great Northern, Seymour Clarke had introduced day return tickets for 1st and 2nd class travel between any two stations on the line. These tickets, issued at three-quarters of the price of two singles, were a bargain for those eager to travel, particularly as services on the line were expanded.

In 1857 the menacing confederacy faltered and came to its end. At last the young Great Northern was entering a period of relative calm and prosperity and could embark on a policy of expansion. That very year, 1857, had seen an agreement concluded between the G.N. and the Manchester, Sheffield and Lincolnshire Railways for the Great Northern to operate through express services from King's Cross to Manchester. In spite of continued hostility from the L.N.W. expressing itself this time in the harassment of passengers who had travelled on the rival train, the G.N. Manchester 'flyers' became established and were to rank among the fastest trains in the country.

In 1864, the year in which Edmund Denison retired, the company was promoting a bill for the ownership of the Leeds, Bradford and Halifax, and the West Yorkshire Railways. In 1865, under the new chairman, Colonel Packe, negotiations were under way with the M.S. and L. for joint ownership of the West Riding and Grimsby line. The following year, the Cheshire Lines Committee was formed to build a group of lines in L.N.W. territory, to be owned by the Midland, the Great Northern and the Manchester, Sheffield and Lincolnshire Railways. The Lincolnshire loop line was completed in 1867 and twelve years later an agreement was finally concluded between the G.N. and the Great Eastern, in E. Anglia, to build a line from Lincoln to Spalding and to put the whole line from Doncaster to Huntingdon via Lincoln, Spalding and March into joint ownership. It was also in the 1870s that the G.N.

10 A typical Great Northern main line vehicle of around 1910, with the luxury of twelve wheels.

began to develop its Enfield commuter services, by building extra lines and new stations, and issuing season tickets to the regular travellers. There were of course still difficulties to be faced. In 1872, for example, the G.N. was excluded by exorbitant rates from transporting Midlands coal, via Grantham to London. Coal being an important mineral on the G.N. line, the company took the decision to lay its own track to the Midlands mines from Colwick, via Derby, and on to join the North Staffordshire railway. The decision was to prove useful in more ways than one, for in 1881 the G.N. was able to buy the Stafford-Uttoxeter railway and use its Colwick-Derby line for through passenger services to Stafford.

By this date, G.N. passenger trains travelled far and wide. They reached York and Harrogate by running powers over the North Eastern metals; they reached Manchester by courtesy of the M.S.L Railway; they reached Liverpool over the Cheshire lines, and they reached Yarmouth and Lowestoft via the Midland and Great Northern Joint line.

The Great Northern is perhaps best remembered, however, for its part in the East Coast London–Scottish express service. Beginning in 1850 on the Lincolnshire loop line, the G.N. ran one Scottish express a day. By 1910 it was running six Scottish express trains between 10 a.m. and 11.30 p.m. daily. Trains leaving King's Cross at 10 a.m. and travelling on the main northern line would be in York by 1.37 p.m. Here they would be handed over to the North Eastern company for the journey to Edinburgh and then to the North British company for the run to Aberdeen.

The speeds of the Scottish express trains had been very greatly improved as a direct result of the celebrated railway races, to Edinburgh in 1888, and to Aberdeen in 1895, between the East and West Coast companies. In 1887, the Great Northern Railway and its allies on the East Coast route to Scotland were taking passengers from London to Edinburgh in 9 hours, whilst the L.N.W. and its ally on the West, were taking 10 hours for the same journey. By 1888 the West Coast companies had equalled the East and got their London to Edinburgh running time down to 9 hours. Such competition the East Coast companies would not take lying down and they therefore reduced their running time to 8½ hours. Whereupon, the West Coast group announced that it, too, would take its passengers from the English to the Scottish capital in 8½ hours. But on the very day it set out to do it the East Coast express managed the journey in 8 hours. The racing had really begun in earnest, each side in turn reducing the time taken to travel from London to Edinburgh, ending in the East Coast's splendid achievement of 7 hours 32 minutes. The result of this exciting competition was an agreed timing of 8¼ hours to Edinburgh by both routes.

11 The first Gresley Pacific. The third, 'Flying Scotsman' appeared new in L.N.E.R. colours in 1923. There were eventually well over 100 of this basic type. Gresley received a knighthood and the 100th was built and named 'Sir Nigel Gresley'. It was one of the streamlined engines, and is now privately preserved.

The truce between the two sides lasted uneasily for seven years. Then, in 1895, there was another bout of racing fever, this time affecting the Aberdeen traffic and resulting in the East Coast's time for the London to Aberdeen run being cut from 11 hours 35 minutes to 8 hours 40 minutes.

The engines most used for the Great Northern's part in both these races were the famous 'eight footers' evolved by Patrick Stirling, the G.N. locomotive superintendent from 1866 to 1895. These engines, finished in the company's light green livery, lined with black and white, were among the first to be built at the G.N. locomotive works at Doncaster. For many years after its formation, it had been the practice of the G.N. to buy its locomotives from outside builders, and it was not until the advent of Stirling that the first locomotives were built by the company. Subsequently many noteworthy engines were produced at Doncaster, including, long after the grouping, *Mallard*, holder of the world speed record for steam locomotives, and basically a Great Northern design.

The Great Northern was reaching its zenith at the time of the race to Aberdeen in 1895. Goods traffic, of bricks, iron, cattle, and especially coal from South Yorkshire and the Midlands, was an important aspect of the company's business, by 1910 amounting to 21 million tons carried annually. The marshalling yards at Doncaster, Colwick and Peterborough had all been rebuilt and enlarged to deal with the growing volume of traffic, and the speed of the G.N. goods trains had been increased enormously. One of the most outstanding of the Great Northern's goods 'expresses' was the King's Cross to Manchester train, which fully laden, covered the distance in 5 hours 50 minutes. The G.N. was also among the foremost in installing traffic control for its goods lines, and by 1914 the whole network of track was served by a system of control telephones.

Promotion of coastal holiday resorts on the G.N. line was also undertaken in earnest. Skegness was the object of a massive publicity campaign; the G.N. offering to take passengers from King's Cross to the bracing seaside air for a return fare of only three shillings. The passenger services to the West Riding of Yorkshire and to the Midlands were swift and frequent, and the organisation of traffic for the St. Leger Day races was masterly.

The Great Northern, beset by early difficulties, had never actually reached York on its own metals. Many of its main line stations were unpretentious, and the company was one of the few in this country not to own or operate steamers to Continental ports. Yet in spite of all this, the Great Northern in many respects did live up to its name. This was particularly so where the London–Scottish passenger traffic was concerned, and it was largely the Great Northern tradition which was to be carried over into the London and North Eastern Railway company, when the third Gresley 'Pacific' locomotive was actually named *Flying Scotsman*—the name so long (though at first unofficially) associated with the 10 a.m. express which had been leaving King's Cross at that time for sixty years past.

London and North Western Railway.

THE POPULAR ROUTE

FROM

London (Euston) to Manchester	in 3 hrs. 30 min.	London (Euston) to Edinburgh	in 8 hrs. 15 min.
" " Liverpool	in 3 hrs. 35 min.	" " to Glasgow	in 8 hrs. 15 min.
" " Birmingham	in 2 hrs. 0 min.	" " to Aberdeen	in 11 hrs. 28 min.
" " Dublin (via Holyhead)	in 9 hrs. 0 min.	" " to Belfast (via Fleetwood)	in 12 hrs. 15 min.

SLEEPING SALOONS ON THE NIGHT TRAINS.

BREAKFAST, LUNCHEON, TEA AND DINING CARS ARE RUN ON THE PRINCIPAL TRAINS.

West Coast Express.

ROYAL MAIL ROUTE BETWEEN ENGLAND AND SCOTLAND, WALES AND IRELAND.

EXPRESS PASSENGER ROUTES BETWEEN ENGLAND & IRELAND

Via Holyhead and Dublin (North Wall).
" Holyhead and Kingstown.
" Holyhead and Greenore.

Via Fleetwood and Belfast.
" Liverpool and Belfast.
" Carlisle, Stranraer, and Larne.

Comfortable Hotels at Euston (London), Bletchley, Birmingham (New Street), Crewe, Edinburgh (Princes Street).

L. & N.W. Steamer leaving Holyhead Harbour.

Comfortable Hotels at Liverpool (Lime Street), Preston, Holyhead, Greenore, Dublin, Glasgow (Central).

Express Through Goods Trains have been established for the expeditious conveyance of General Merchandise and Live Stock; also Fruit, Fish, Meat, Game, and other Perishable Goods, giving quick travel and prompt delivery.

Euston Station, London,

FRANK REE, General Manager

12 L.N.W.R. magazine publicity, 1914.

MAJOR ROUTES OF THE LONDON AND NORTH WESTERN RAILWAY

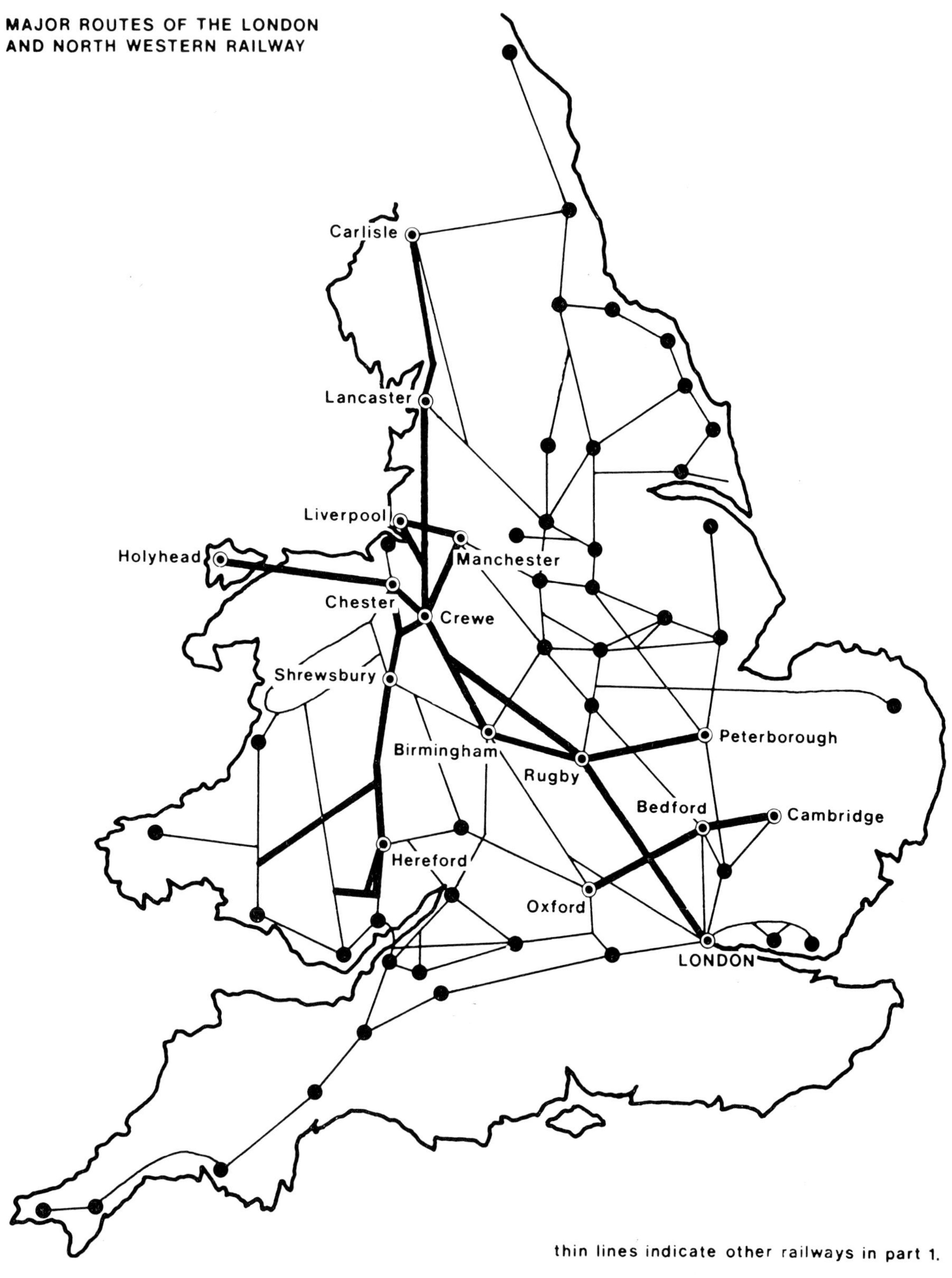

thin lines indicate other railways in part 1.

The London and North Western Railway

13 The London and Birmingham Railway at Chalk Farm, *c.* 1840. The train looks curiously primitive and toylike, but the farm is already overshadowed by the spreading metropolis.

On 15 September 1830 the Liverpool and Manchester Railway was opened by the Duke of Wellington, then prime minister. Compared with the rustic celebrations on the Stockton and Darlington five years earlier, this was a great National occasion, for in five years the public railway had come far in public esteem. The Liverpool and Manchester was a main line railway, the first part of the country's main line network to be built. It was engineered by George Stephenson and was a masterpiece of civil engineering, particularly in the way in which the peat bog of Chat Moss had been made to support the track.

Sixteen years later the L. & M.R. became part of the London and North Western, a railway which was to become the largest joint stock corporation in the country and to earn itself the title of 'The Premier Line'. Also incorporated in the new L.N.W.R. were the London and Birmingham and Grand Junction railways, dating from 1837, and taken together they provided a trunk route from London to the Midlands and north west. Thus the new company could claim a distinguished provenance, not as historic as that of the North Eastern after it had absorbed the Stockton and Darlington, but second to none other.

The L.N.W.R. eventually became a substantial empire, stretching from London in the south to Carlisle in the north, and from Swansea in the west to Cambridge in the east. Not surprisingly, its senior officers conducted themselves like emperors, autocratic within their empire and cunning in their diplomatic relations with other powers. They were not always successful in their attempts to forestall competition, but the company paid its shareholders well.

The empire was not closely knit in its early years. There were, for instance, two railway works: a northern works at Crewe, and a southern at Wolverton. Crewe painted its engines green, and Wolverton used a fiery red. Eventually Wolverton was turned into the carriage works, and from there came the most elegant and luxurious of all British railway carriages—for the more opulent passenger on the more important routes—including sumptuous saloons for the Royal Family and the Duke of Sutherland. These lovely carriages were more than extravagant expressions of pomp and circumstance, they were works of art. Happily, they are preserved in the York Railway Museum.

Crewe had a great tradition of engineering, and a locomotive type especially associated with it, though built for many other railways. One of the first presiding engineers was Francis Trevithick, son of the inventor of the steam locomotive, and it was under his superintendence that the 'Crewe' or 'Allan' type was built. *Columbine* in the Railway Museum at York is an early example. John Ramsbottom developed Crewe works into the most complete railway works in the country, and there some of the most successful engineers of other railways received their training. Ramsbottom built an excellent light 2-2-2 express type, the 'Problem' or 'Lady of the Lake' class, which did splendid work in the 1888 race to Edinburgh, though then quite an old type yet valued for its dependability. He also created the 'DX' goods design, which was mass produced in over 900 examples, and which survived in various rebuilt states well into the period after 1923.

The best express engines built at Wolverton were the 'Bloomers' designed by J. E. McConnell, considerably more powerful than Ramsbottom's engines and possibly, in their bold red livery, designed to put Crewe out of countenance. Rivalry of this kind was very much part of the railway way of life, even in the days of the group railways, and the L.N.W.R., being itself a sort of 'group' in the middle of the nineteenth century, was not immune. The 'Bloomers' were quite outstanding engines but after McConnell's retirement in 1862, Wolverton built no more locomotives.

Ramsbottom's successor at Crewe was F. W. Webb, an engineer who showed the highest qualities as an organiser, and a very able locomotive designer as long as he followed Ramsbottom's lead. As the latter remained for many years on the board of the L.N.W.R. Webb had little alternative, but when he did develop truly original designs he produced a long series of ill-conceived compound locomotives, only a few of which happened to do some good work. The compound locomotive had been successfully launched by Anatole Mallet in France in 1876, and was to prove notably successful on the Continent. But because of Webb's prestige as chief mechanical engineer of the great L.N.W.R. the feeling became widespread in Britain that if Webb could not build a good compound locomotive, such a thing could not be built at all. This was something of a tragedy for locomotive engineering in Britain.

14 One of F. W. Webb's impressive but temperamental three-cylinder compound locomotives for the L.N.W.R., 1885.

15 London and North Western postal train. Note the folded nets on some of the coaches, and the corridor vestibules at the sides of the coach ends, to prevent coupling up to normal passenger stock, with possible access by unauthorised persons.

However, Webb's best design was the brilliant 2-4-0 type known as the 'Jumbos', based on something similar but smaller by Ramsbottom, and one of these, now in the York Railway Museum, was *Hardwicke*, which produced an altogether remarkable power output, for so small a machine, during the celebrated railway races to the north. In many ways, this class set the style that was to see the L.N.W.R. through to the grouping. Simple in conception, plain in finish, uncomfortable to ride upon, cheap to build, pleasing to the eye in an austere way and finished in shiny black, L.N.W.R. engines were notable for vigorous performance quite out of keeping with their modest size. It would be hard to imagine anything more completely in contrast with the masterful luxury of the engines of the North Eastern, yet they did their job. They quite often did it in pairs, and L.N.W.R. locos of later years did not last as long as those of the North Eastern, but there was nothing wrong with their economics.

George Whale succeeded Webb in 1903, and rapidly disposing of Webb's later engines, based his 4-4-0 'Precursor' class on the 'Jumbos'. C. J. Bowen Cooke produced a superheated version, of which the most famous was *Coronation*, the 5000th locomotive built at Crewe, in 1911. And elegance was finally achieved with the larger four-cylinder 4-6-0 type of which the first was no. 2222, *Sir Gilbert Claughton*—one of those euphonious or challenging names of railway dignitaries which were the twentieth century's substitute for the *Hercules*, *Samson*, or *Colossus* of the early days of the locomotive.

Euston Station was the immensely dignified headquarters of the Premier Line, wherein trains of off-white and purple-brown carriages waited, behind shining blue-black locomotives, for the 'right away' from splendidly uniformed officials. Among these trains, and an essential part of the corporate image of the L.N.W.R., were the special postal expresses, their carriages equipped with folding nets to catch the mails hung beside the line, as the train swept past. These carriages also shed similar leather pouches of Royal Mail to nets upon the ground, as the postal sorters worked away at the vast nests of pigeon holes which lined their interiors. The travelling post office was not confined to the L.N.W.R. (though the West Coast route held the Royal warrant for the Scottish mail) and it is still a feature of our railways in a simplified form. But the 'West Coast Postal', and the 'Irish Mail' epitomised the position of the L.N.W.R. as a national institution and a public service.

The year 1846 saw the formation of this London and North Western Railway Company, by the amalgamation of the Grand Junction Railway, which had opened in 1837, the Liverpool and Manchester of 1830, and the London and Birmingham Railway, engineered by Robert Stephenson and opened in 1837, together with the Manchester and Birmingham Railway which ran via Stockport and joined the Grand Junction at Crewe.

These companies had by 1846 already absorbed smaller lines. The Grand Junction had taken in the Liverpool and Manchester, the Chester and Crewe, the Leigh and Kenyon, and the Bolton and Leigh Railways, while the London and Birmingham had taken over, amongst others, the Warwick and Leamington, the Rugby and Leamington, and the Bedford Railways. Such were the first constituents of the L.N.W. An arrangement was soon concluded, however, between the L.N.W. and the Lancashire and Yorkshire Railway, concerning their joint ownership of the Preston and Wigan line, part of the North Union Railway, which connected with the West Coast route from London.

One London and North Western main line, therefore ran from London, Euston, via Birmingham and Newton to Preston. Thence, by running powers over the metals of the Preston and Lancaster Railway and the newly opened Lancaster and Carlisle Railway, London and North Western trains reached the Scottish border. An agreement with the Caledonian Railway company in 1848 gave the L.N.W. direct access to Edinburgh and Glasgow.

The Preston and Lancaster, and Lancaster and Carlisle Railways were eventually taken over on lease by the L.N.W. in 1859. Meanwhile in 1847, the North Western's route from London had been shortened by some nine miles, with the completion of the Trent Valley Railway, running from Rugby to Stafford.

16 The first of the 'George the Fifth' type, 1910. This superheated type proved phenomenally powerful for its size, with the result that the class was habitually overworked and wore out prematurely.

The lines branching to left and right of the L.N.W. main northern line ran originally to Bedford, Leamington, Chester, Liverpool and Manchester, but new branch lines were constantly being added to the network, until it had become one of the largest in the country.

Eastwards, North Western lines ran to Leeds, with the absorption of the Leeds, Dewsbury and Manchester Railway in 1847, to Cambridge via Bedford, with the absorption of that line in 1865, and to Peterborough, with the construction of a new line from Rugby, opened in 1850.

Westwards, the Buckinghamshire Railways with a line to Oxford, and the Shropshire Union Railway with its line from Stafford to Shrewsbury, were both leased to the London and North Western in 1847. The Chester and Holyhead Railway, employing L.N.W. stock from its opening in 1850, was finally absorbed into the company in 1858. Further L.N.W. inroads were made into Wales until the absorption of the Central Wales line in 1868, the Anglesey Central line in 1876, the Central Wales and Carmarthen Junction 1891, the Merthyr, Tredegar and Abergavenny Railway in 1866 and the Brynmawr and Blaenavon Railway in 1869. These last two plus several joint ownership agreements with the Great Western Railway Company gave the L.N.W. access to the rich coal mining areas of South Wales.

Captain Mark Huish, the energetic first general manager of the L.N.W., did much to set the company on its feet, but it was during the Chairmanship of Richard Moon (1861–91) that the London and North Western began to acquire its distinctive character and to build up its tradition of independence and service. Moon's economy drives helped; for by 1870, Moon had been able to reduce expenditure in working the line from 71% to 47% of the receipts, the profits so acquired being ploughed back into the company.

To cope with the increasing traffic and to improve operating efficiency, various improvements were made to the line. The track between Stafford and Crewe was made quadruple in 1873 and a loop line was built around the engine works at Crewe, to permit unhindered through running. A direct line from Liverpool, south, via Runcorn, was begun in 1869, and a new line from Bletchley to Rugby via Northampton was completed in 1862.

It was also whilst Richard Moon held the reins of the L.N.W. that the Crewe engine works, opened in 1843 by the Grand Junction Railway, developed into something peculiarly London and North Western. In 1862, with the appointment of John

Ramsbottom to the newly created post of Chief Mechanical Engineer, the Northern and Southern locomotive divisions were amalgamated. Wolverton became the centre for carriage construction only, and Crewe the centre for locomotive construction. Ramsbottom straightway gained permission to build a Bessemer steel works at Crewe so that the L.N.W. could make its own rails, its own locomotives and, from 1873 onwards, its own signals, from the raw materials; and was the only railway company to do so much of its own manufacturing.

The passenger services of the L.N.W. were extensive and on the whole efficient. The main passenger express routes ran from London to Birmingham, London to Manchester and London to Liverpool where connection was made with the transatlantic steamers, bound for New York; Liverpool being in fact the main port for sailings to America until the South Western Railway Company began to develop Southampton in the 1890s. From 1848, in conjunction with the Caledonian company began perhaps the best remembered of all L.N.W. express services, those from London to Edinburgh and Glasgow. There was, however, from 1850 hot competition for this traffic, from the parallel East Coast Anglo-Scottish services, a competition which eventually produced the famous and sometimes hair-raising races to Scotland of 1888 and 1895.

The L.N.W. also took its passengers to Wales and Ireland. Swansea, Carmarthen and the coastal resorts of North Wales were all served by L.N.W. trains, and with the absorption of the Chester and Holyhead Railway, the London and North Western had gained a port from which it could run its own steamers to Ireland. From Holyhead, L.N.W. vessels plied to North Wall, Kingstown and Greenore, rivalling the ships of the Dublin Steam Packet Company, which, although primarily concerned with the shipment of mail, also carried passengers. But that was not all, for in conjunction with the Lancashire and Yorkshire Railway, the L.N.W. also worked with the shipment of mail, also carried passengers. But that was not all, for in conjunction with the Lancashire and Yorkshire railway, the L.N.W. also worked steamers from Fleetwood, so offering the swiftest passage to Belfast.

The company had an early reputation for friendliness and courtesy in its dealings with the public, partly through the efforts of R. Creed, one of its first secretaries, and it was soon to gain admiration for the smartness of its uniformed staff. Its standards in passenger comfort varied; sometimes directly with the need to attract custom from rival concerns. Some of the L.N.W. stations, such as those at Oxenholme and Carnforth, on the Lancaster and Carlisle line, did not offer comfort of a very high standard, and much of the rolling-stock used by the company, in the twentieth century at least, was old although usually clean.

The company excelled, however, in fostering passenger comfort on some of its main express lines. The all-corridor trains introduced in 1897 for the London–Scottish routes were famous in this respect, being luxuriously fitted, wider than previous stock and seating only two a side, in the first class. The coaches of the 'American Specials' of 1907, built for the Liverpool service, set an even higher standard of comfort, and were followed the next year by a new set of similar stock for the Scottish services. These were 65 feet long, with 12 wheels, as against the previous standard of 57 feet length and eight wheels, and gave an even smoother ride, partly

17 *Sir Gilbert Claughton* and the two-colour coaches epitomise the real elegance of L.N.W.R. trains at their stateliest.

because of attention to brakes and couplings which allowed little in the way of jolting and jerking when starting and stopping. Inside, even the third-class seats were upholstered in black and crimson velvet.

In the matter of speed, the company had for very many years believed in the 40 mile an hour express train, under the guidance of Richard Moon who saw speed as giving rise to discomfort and expense. The railway races to Edinburgh and Aberdeen, in 1888 and 1895, put an end to the old way of thinking, at least as far as the principal trains were concerned. Part of the trouble had been that the locomotives were underpowered, and the cure for that, in Webb's time at least, and indeed frequently into L.M.S. days, was to put two engines at the head of the train. Even the excellent engines built in the twentieth century were underpowered for the very heavy and luxurious trains which made up more and more of the express formations.

The freight locomotives were better matched to their tasks. There were large numbers of very good 0-6-0 engines of Ramsbottom and Webb design, and the Webb eight-coupled compound goods locomotives of various types were fully capable of taking the heaviest trains, and after rebuilding were still to be found on similar duties in the days of nationalisation.

As with practically all main line railways, the transportation of goods was the main business of the L.N.W.R., with its strategic branches running to the West Riding, Holyhead, South Wales and even Cambridgeshire. Coal was carried all over the system, and there were special traffics like that in livestock from Ireland. In 1910 the company carried 55 million tons of freight consignments and, incidentally, 77 million passenger journeys were made in its trains.

When this largest British railway joined the L.M.S. group in 1923 it had gone a long way towards bringing the whole system up to twentieth-century standards. The vast complex of Crewe—the workshops, the marshalling yards, and the station—had been reorganised and by-passing tracks provided for through traffic. The riverside station at Liverpool, and the adjoining part of the Mersey, had been adapted to take the largest liners, in an effort to counter the attractions of Southampton, which was being developed by the L.S.W.R. The North London Railway, long a satellite of the L.N.W.R., had been assimilated with the major system and its City terminus at Broad Street brought into use for some main line trains, while its commuter services, together with those of the L.N.W.R. proper, were electrified using rolling-stock which echoed the magnificence of Wolverton's express stock. Lastly, in a final coup before the grouping, the L.N.W.R. had amalgamated with the substantial Lancashire and Yorkshire Railway, long a close associate but nevertheless a major British railway and hitherto an independent one.

At the grouping, this proud company suffered a considerable humiliation. The dominant partner in the new group was the Midland. How this happened is a long story, but it must be admitted that the Midland supremacy in the councils of the London, Midland and Scottish was not wholly undeserved. But the painting of the purple-brown and off-white carriages in Midland red was a sad symbol as well as an aesthetic mistake, even though the North Western locomotives wore the Midland red extremely well. Twenty-five years later, at nationalisation, the spirit of the L.N.W.R., still active on the railway, was appeased by the spectacle of the famous Midland compounds freshly painted in a new livery—the 'intermediate passenger' livery of British Railways—which was none other than the L.N.W.R. black, with red, cream and grey lining!

18 Pre-grouping railways had their individual styles of signal, too. This is the approach to Rugby on the L.N.W.R.

G. W. R.

When The Railway News first appeared the Great Western had only 1,450 miles of railway—to-day it has over 3,000. 50 years of progress and prosperity have made the G.W.R. Britain's most up-to-date Railway. Its Train Services, both as regards speed and comfort, are acknowledged to be amongst the best in the World. You will enjoy travelling if you go "Great Western"—the line for smooth running.

THE SHORTEST ROUTES.

LONDON—BIRMINGHAM via Bicester.
ENGLAND—IRELAND via Fishguard.

HOLIDAY BOOKS OF THE HOLIDAY LINE.

The travel books published by the G.W.R. have become widely known as "The Holiday Books of the Holiday Line." They are unique in railway literature, and form an exceedingly popular series of literary handbooks owing to the thoroughly practical, and at the same time interesting, manner in which the information is presented. All the travel books are printed in best style, beautifully illustrated, and each contains an excellent map. :: ::

LIST OF TRAVEL BOOKS.

THE CORNISH RIVIERA. Price 3d., post free 6d.

New edition in course of preparation.

DEVON: THE SHIRE OF THE SEA KINGS. Price 3d., post free 6d.

SOUTHERN IRELAND: ITS LAKES AND LANDSCAPES: Price 3d., post free 6d.

"Both dainty and artistic. . . . Fully illustrated by reproductions of charming photographs."—"Madame."

WONDERFUL WESSEX: Wilts, Somerset and Dorset. Price 6d., post free 10d.

"Most comprehensive and splendidly illustrated . . . invaluable to tourists. The Great Western Railway Company is to be congratulated upon the production of so complete a guide."—"Daily Mirror."

HISTORIC SITES AND SCENES OF ENGLAND. For Travellers of all Nations. Price 3d., post free 6d.

RURAL LONDON: The Chalfont Country and the Thames Valley. Price 3d., post free 6d.

SOUTH WALES: THE COUNTRY OF CASTLES. Price 3d., post free 6d.

New edition in course of preparation.

NORTH WALES: The British Tyrol. Price 3d., post free, 6d.

HOMES FOR ALL: London's Western Borderlands. A residential guide and property register. Issued quarterly. Free. Postage 3d.

HOMES FOR ALL: In Rural Birmingham. A residential guide and property register. Issued quarterly. Free. Postage 3d.

The travel books may be obtained at the Company's principal stations and offices at the prices shewn, or will be forwarded on application to the Superintendent of the Line's Office, G.W.R., PADDINGTON STATION, LONDON, W., on receipt of stamps :: :: :: ::

G.W.R. THE HOLIDAY LINE.

FRANK POTTER, General Manager.

19 Great Western magazine publicity, 1914. The locomotive is one of Churchward's four-cylinder 'Star' class.

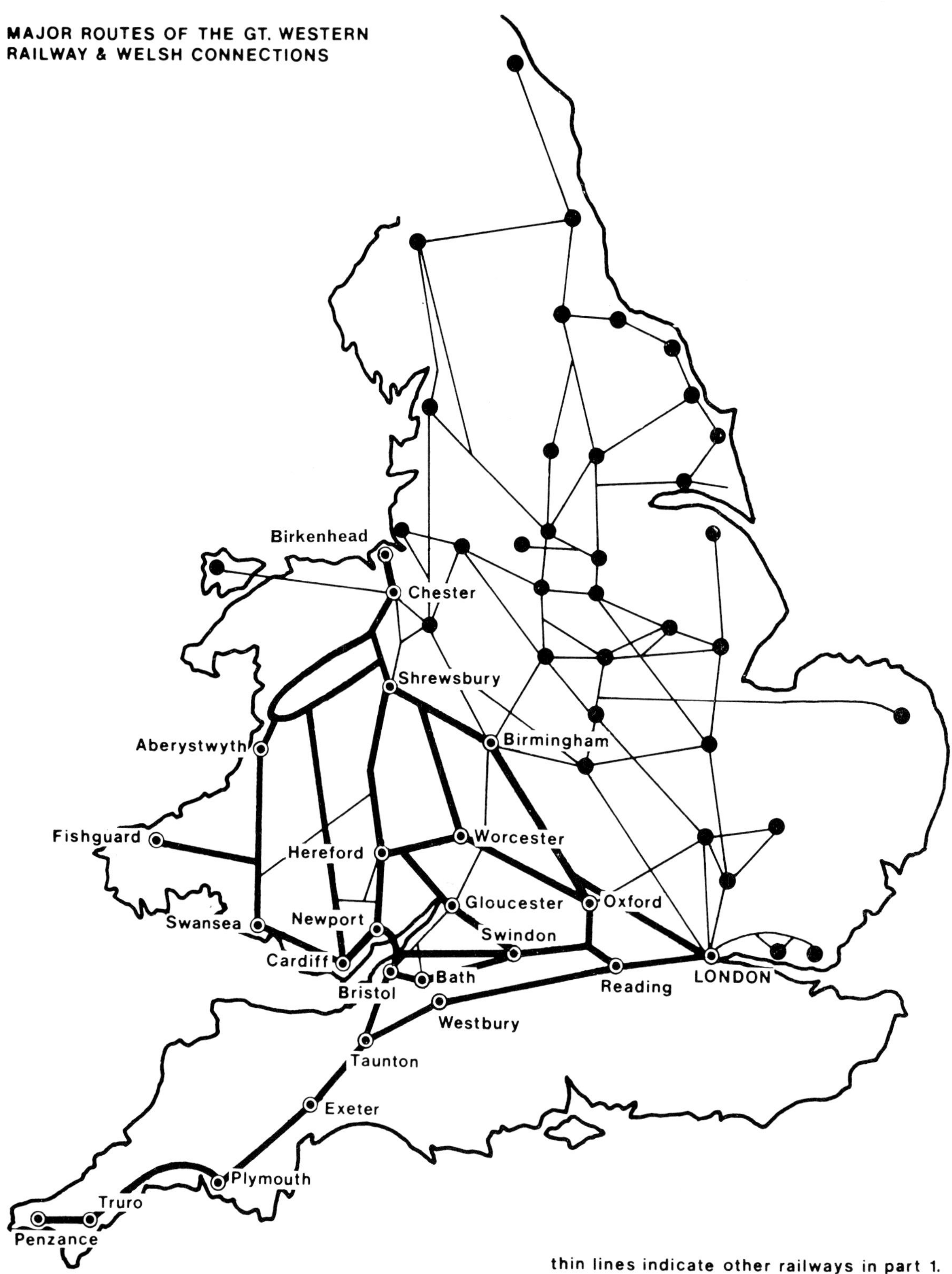
MAJOR ROUTES OF THE GT. WESTERN
RAILWAY & WELSH CONNECTIONS
Birkenhead
Chester
Shrewsbury
Aberystwyth
Birmingham
Fishguard
Hereford
Worcester
Swansea
Newport
Gloucester
Oxford
Swindon
Cardiff
Bath
Bristol
Reading
LONDON
Westbury
Taunton
Exeter
Plymouth
Truro
Penzance
thin lines indicate other railways in part 1.

The Great Western Railway

Of all the pre-grouping companies, the old Great Western was the one with the personality best known today. This is because, at the grouping, instead of being joined to a few other large companies, it was joined to numerous small ones. Of these only six were classed as constituents, and of the six only four were of any size: the Barry, Cambrian, Rhymney, and Taff Vale Railways. The Taff Vale was the largest and most prosperous of these. An extremely busy and ably run railway, it had been founded in 1836, less than a year after the Great Western itself, and at the height of its operations it handled over 8 million tons of goods (mainly coal) and 8 million passengers per year, and paid a dividend of 17½%. At its amalgamation with the G.W.R., which took place one year before the general grouping date, it had 112 miles of route and 275 locomotives.

The Cambrian Railways were a very different concern, with 300 miles of rural lines threading the beautiful scenery of mid-Wales. This was never a prosperous company though it ran some creditable expresses along its predominantly single-track main lines. One of these expresses was involved with a local train in a sensational head-on collision at Abermule in 1921, and the memory of this tragedy is still very alive in mid-Wales. A more happy association of the Cambrian is that narrow gauge line which runs up the Vale of Rheidol from Aberystwyth, and now the only part of British Railways to be operated by steam locomotives.

In addition to the six constituent companies, the Great Western acquired 12 subsidiary companies, all but two in South Wales. One of the two exceptions, the Midland and South Western Junction Railway, was a rural line about 60 miles long, which ran from Cheltenham to Andover, via Swindon, with running powers all the way to Southampton. Though never very busy, it enjoyed a useful strategic position in the railway system and provided the Great Western stronghold of Swindon with the impudent spectacle of red locomotives, eventually to be painted in the proper Swindon green after the grouping.

The old Great Western was a spectacular railway. I. K. Brunel had conceived its engineering in the grand manner, with the celebrated broad gauge of 7 feet and large bore tunnels, which enabled it, even after the last of the broad gauge tracks had been removed in 1892, to run trains which were noticeably higher and wider than elsewhere in Great Britain. Brunel also endowed it with some splendid bridges, of which that spanning the Tamar at Saltash is the most celebrated and is now, in a literal sense, his memorial, his name being writ large in letters of stone upon it.

There was, around the turn of the century, a remarkable change of character. The letters G.W.R. had at one time been popularly interpreted as 'Great Way Round', and this was a fair comment on the way the G.W.R. reached its destinations. The locomotives before Churchward's time were of noble and powerful aspect, but with a suggestion of the Dinosaur about them: a reflection of the fact that Gooch's magnificent broad gauge engines had hardly changed in half a century, and Dean's narrow gauge ones had been planned to be convertible from the broad gauge, even his later designs reflecting this onetime necessity. The boast of heraldry was conspicuous on them, and the pomp of power symbolized by the most enormous polished brass domes upon their boilers. There was also elegance, in the light iron-work of the transepted roof at Paddington, in the stone buildings of country stations, and in the cream and brown panelled coaches with airy clerestoried roofs, the compartment doors of which shut with a quiet click which immediately excluded the bustling sounds of the station from their comfortable interiors.

The great change came when new and shorter routes were built to cut off the corners of the old system, when Churchward produced a new standard range of starkly modern-looking locomotives, when huge carriages called 'Dreadnoughts' appeared on the best expresses, and when these were painted dark red all over. This last change was unequivocally for the worse, and happily did not last long. Chocolate and cream carriages were a Great Western trademark, and to paint them in a shade which could belong to the North Eastern, the North British, or even the South Eastern and Chatham, was poor public relations.

The grand manner did not lessen with the change. The 70-foot carriages were matched in 1908 by the first British 'Pacific', suitably named *The Great Bear*. It remained the only example of its type, rather too big even for the high speeds and heavy trains of the changed Great Western, but it was a highly successful piece of engineering, and of publicity. The harsh lines of Churchward's earlier locomotives were modified by the addition of a few stately curves, and cast-iron chimneys gave way to ones of traditional G.W.R. pattern with copper caps. More polished brass, reminiscent of the days of Dean, eventually made the engines as handsome as any that ever ran on a British railway.

But quite apart from the physical apparatus of transport, a railway derives much of its character from the places it serves, and their associations. Brunel saw the Great Western not merely as serving Bristol and London, but as the route to the New World. The *Great Western* steamship was an extension of the railway. But in fact, despite occasional moments of grandeur at Bristol, Plymouth, or Fishguard, the transoceanic railways were the London and North Western and the London and South Western. The character of the Great Western had in fact three facets, and of these the most important was the South Wales connection. Welsh voices were to be heard at Paddington, and coal trains ran briskly from west to east. A second facet, very much in evidence at Paddington, was the academic, clerical, ladylike and gentlemanly air of the many passengers for Oxford, Hereford, Worcester, Cheltenham and Bath. Lastly, but predominantly in the mind of most of the public, if Great Western publicity was effective, this was the railway which went to the west country, to Devon and Cornwall—to the Cornish Riviera where the names were as exotic and the sun benign as in Italy, which, the posters declared, was even the same shape as Cornwall. How remote all this was from the ideas of the founders will soon become apparent.

The Great Western Railway began officially in August 1835 with a proposal to build one double line from London to Bristol for the benefit of the merchant

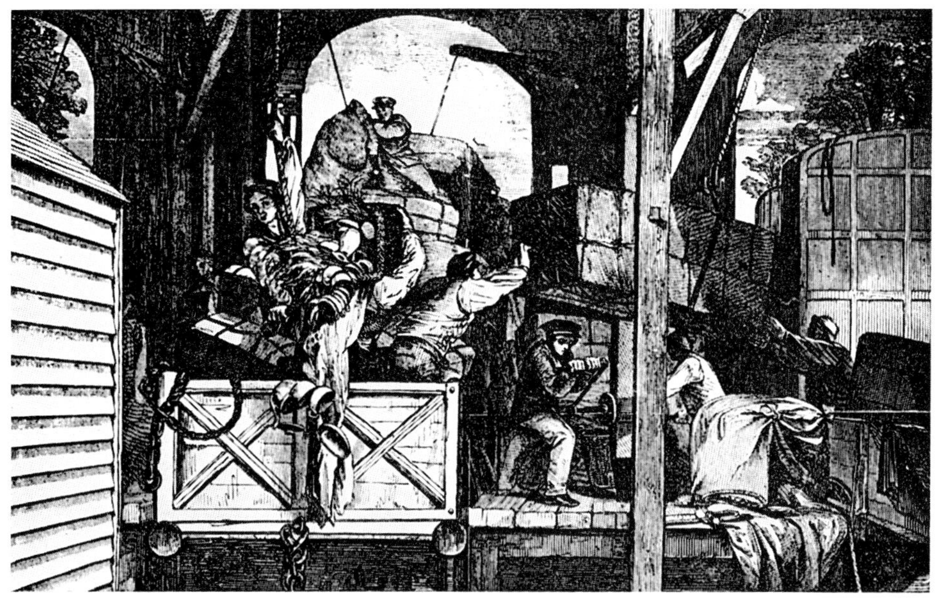

20 Trans-shipment of goods from the broad to the standard gauge.

community. With Charles A. Saunders as secretary to the company and the eccentric Isambard Kingdom Brunel as engineer, the new G.W.R. soon abandoned all previous ideas of sharing Euston station with the London and Birmingham Railway and instead began laying its own separate and quite distinctive broad gauge track from a temporary London terminus at Paddington. (The permanent G.W.R. station at Paddington was not opened until 1854.)

The decision to adopt the 7 ft. broad gauge line as opposed to the more usual 4 ft. 8½ ins., was taken by the G.W. board as early as October 1835 and was characteristic of the individuality of the company. Brunel was the originator and chief protagonist of this broad gauge, believing it to be easier for trains to run faster on such a track and safer for passengers to travel in coaches hung between the carriage wheels. There was little concrete evidence to support these beliefs and the coaches built to the 'carriage between the wheels' design proved quite unpopular, but nevertheless the 7-ft. gauge, through the sheer enthusiasm of Brunel and Saunders, made remarkable progress in the early years of the company.

The original Great Western line, broad gauge throughout, was opened in 1841, and ran to Bristol via Didcot, Swindon and Chippenham. Two years later the company bought the Cheltenham and Great Western Union Railway which ran from Swindon to Cheltenham, and converted this to the broad gauge. Thereupon the Bristol and Gloucester Railway, then linked with the G.W.R. at both ends of its line, felt bound to change its gauge from the standard to the broad, to facilitate the interchange of traffic. Other independent companies in the area, finding a sponsor and supporter in the Great Western, were also well disposed towards building broad gauge lines, and Brunel, foreseeing some kind of broad gauge 'empire', acted as engineer to several of them. It was in this way that the future routes of the Great Western were built and the ground prepared for the expansion of the company.

First came the Bristol and Exeter line via Bridgwater and Taunton. The Bristol and Exeter company had obtained Parliamentary authorisation in 1836, but had then suffered serious financial difficulties. In 1840, its line in a far from completed state was temporarily leased by the Great Western and under these conditions broad gauge track reached Bridgwater in 1841, Taunton in 1842 and Exeter in 1844.

For the Great Western it was a circuitous route from London to Exeter, and not surprisingly Charles Russell as chairman of the company aimed to gain permission for a more direct London–Exeter line, especially so in view of the potential rivalry of the London and South Western Railway with its standard gauge line already at Southampton. The bill proposing the G.W. Exeter direct line did eventually pass through Parliament in 1848, but unfortunately it was too late for the company to raise sufficient funds and the project was allowed to lapse.

Meanwhile broad gauge railway communication was extended westwards from Exeter with the building of the South Devon line, around the coast through Starcross, Dawlish and Teignmouth to Plymouth. To this company the G.W.R. gave a certain amount of financial aid and again Brunel acted as engineer. The line, begun in 1844, was completed to Teignmouth in 1847, to Totnes in 1848 and to Plymouth in 1849, and saw the early inauguration, and failure, of atmospheric traction.

Outside the South West, the broad gauge was simultaneously making inroads into Wales. The South Wales company, authorised in 1845, was from the start sponsored by the Great Western, quick to see the advantages of the line with its proposed outlet to Ireland. The original plan was for a line from Chepstow via Cardiff, Swansea and Carmarthen to Fishguard, with an additional act of 1846 authorising the extension to Gloucester for the link with the G.W.R. By 1852, broad gauge track had reached Carmarthen, but the South Wales company, then short of funds, could go no further and it was left to the Pembroke and Tenby junction railway to take the track to Pembroke, still on the broad gauge. Not until the twentieth century, long after the South Wales line had been absorbed by the G.W.R., was the railway completed to Fishguard.

During the first decade or so of the Great Western's history, the broad gauge had enjoyed reasonable success: but opposition was growing and in 1845 a Royal Commission on Railway Gauges was set up to enquire into the trouble caused by the break of gauge at Gloucester, the Bristol and Gloucester Railway being broad gauge, the Gloucester and Birmingham standard gauge. A specially exaggerated display of the difficulties involved in changing from one gauge to the next was staged entirely for the benefit of the commission, and not surprisingly the subsequent report was unfavourable to the continuance of the double gauge. This really marked the beginning of the end for the exclusively broad gauge system and for the Brunel–Saunders–Russell concept of the Great Western.

The building of the Oxford and Birmingham line in 1846 was indicative of the new turn of events occasioned by the Railway Commission's report. Beginning as a joint project between the G.W.R. and the Grand Junction Railway, the Oxford and Birmingham ended as an entirely Great Western line, laid not to the broad gauge alone, but to the mixed gauge—that is with three rails instead of two, to enable either broad or standard gauge trains to use it.

21 Brunel's masterpiece and memorial: the Royal Albert Bridge at Saltash, when first completed in 1859.

Moreover, of the three remaining larger independent companies, authorised in 1845 and 1846, which were eventually to become part of the G.W.R. only one was laid exclusively to the broad gauge and that was the Cornwall Railway of 1846 running from Plymouth to Falmouth. Brunel acted as engineer and the line contained perhaps his most famous bridge at Saltash over the Tamar. Shortage of funds meant progress was slow but nevertheless broad gauge track reached Truro in 1859 and Falmouth in 1863. The West Cornwall Railway on the other hand, also of 1846, laid its track to the standard 4 ft. 8½ ins. gauge to incorporate a section of the Hayle Railway already built to that gauge. It was opened from Truro to Penzance in 1852 and laid to the mixed gauge in 1867.

Likewise the Oxford, Worcester and Wolverhampton Railway of 1845, fought over for some years by the Great Western and the London and North Western as to its gauge and suitable working agreements, was finally completed in 1854 as a standard gauge line.

By this time the Great Western was beginning to draw together by absorption the different railway companies of the West Midlands, some standard gauge, some broad gauge. The Shrewsbury and Birmingham, and Shrewsbury and Chester lines which had joined the G.W.R. in 1854 were both standard gauge. The South Wales line which was fully absorbed by the G.W.R. in 1862 was of course broad gauge, but the West Midland Railway, also absorbed by the G.W.R. in 1862 was composed of the Oxford, Worcester and Wolverhampton Railway, the Abergavenny and Hereford line and the Worcester and Hereford line and was standard gauge.

Almost inevitably the question was raised as to the justification of retaining the broad gauge when the majority of other railway companies, and now even a part of the G.W.R., operated on the standard gauge. In 1866 Sir Daniel Gooch, newly elected chairman of the company, put the matter squarely before the G.W. board, and the following year the Royal Commission on Railways recommended that the broad gauge should not be perpetuated.

So it was in 1869 that the new phase in the history of the Great Western began. In that year the 21½-mile line between Hereford and Grange Court was converted from the broad to the standard gauge in 5 days. This was followed in 1872 by the conversion of the entire South Wales main line and for this major undertaking the standard gauge points, crossings and inner curved rails were all made to measure and taken to the appropriate stations along the way before the work began. This enabled the 188 miles of broad gauge double track and the 48 miles of single to be converted to standard gauge in just over three weeks. The Gloucester to Swindon line and numerous branch lines were next on the list and by 1876, the original Great Western Paddington to Bristol main line, if not completely converted, had nevertheless been laid to the mixed gauge.

This left the South West of England as the last stronghold of the broad gauge, a position it was to retain for the next 16 years. The Bristol and Exeter Railway had become a part of the G.W.R. in 1876 and had been laid to the mixed gauge for some years, but the South Devon company which together with the mixed gauge West Cornwall line joined the G.W.R. in 1878, remained broad gauge. So, too, did the Cornwall Railway, and this line, although leased by the G.W.R., was not completely

22 Churchward's eight-coupled mineral engine remained as efficient as any for its class of traffic, right to the end of steam on British Railways, over half a century after its first appearance.

23 At Swindon, Churchward installed the first British stationary locomotive testing plant, seen here with one of his 'Atlantic' engines on the rollers, around 1907.

absorbed until 1889. It was not therefore until 1891 that the decision was taken to bring the broad gauge to a complete end at last. Preparations were made and the work of converting the final stretches of 7 ft. gauge was begun on 20 May 1892. By 23 May 1892 the Great Western was standard gauge throughout.

The task of preparing for and carrying out the gauge conversions of the preceding 30 years had inevitably demanded a sizeable proportion of the company's resources and it was not really until this gauge question had been successfully dealt with that the G.W.R. was able to concentrate its attention on developing its services.

As the track inherited by the G.W.R. from its constituent companies formed a rather meandering network, shortening the main existing routes became one of the the company's top priorities. The $4\frac{1}{2}$-mile long Severn Tunnel, a major feat of engineering, had already been opened in 1886, and a new link line built from Wootton Bassett via Badminton and Chipping Sodbury. 1895 saw plans for a more direct West of England line to run through Patney, Westbury and Castle Cary, and hen the direct Birmingham to Bristol line was made by connecting up a series of branch lines. Finally in conjunction with the Great Central Railway a new line from the G.C.R.'s London extension took G.W.R. trains direct to Birmingham and put them in a position to rival the parallel L.N.W. services.

By the beginning of the twentieth century therefore the G.W.R. was becoming what it had often failed to be before—a really competitive line. To complement the work on shortening the routes, passengers were encouraged to 'Go' Great Western and passenger accommodation was improved. The men responsible for this sustained vitality were led by Viscount Emlyn, a newcomer to the company, elected chairman in 1895. Working with him T. I. Allen, superintendent of the line from 1894 and A. L. Wilkinson, general manager from 1896, had set about streamlining the services of the G.W.R. In an attempt to popularise South Wales as a holiday resort, non-stop train services were begun in 1897 between Cardiff and Paddington and the route advertised as the longest non-stop run in the country. G.W.R. steamer services between New Milford and Waterford in Southern Ireland were promoted between 1898 and 1906 when the G.W.R., having gained control of the Rosslare Railways and Harbour Company, built and opened Fishguard harbour to command one of the shortest routes to Ireland. Accordingly in 1907 trains were running through from Paddington to Fishguard whence one of the new G.W.R. steamers would take passengers in comfort to Rosslare.

The G.W.R. also had early links with transatlantic steamers through I. K. Brunel's *Great Western* built originally to continue the company's passenger services from Bristol. It was therefore a great day for the company when in 1909, so many years later, another transatlantic steamer, the Cunard liner *Mauretania*, called at another, G.W.R. port, Fishguard. Unfortunately for the Great Western, it was only a short-lived arrangement as both the Cunard and the White Star lines were soon to move their terminals to Southampton, but nevertheless for the brief period when Fishguard was a transatlantic terminal the G.W.R. took full advantage, running special express trains to Dover for the continental connections.

The other ocean liner connection of the G.W.R., the non-stop Paddington to Plymouth express of the early twentieth century, was run in competition with the L.S.W.R. and was later extended into Cornwall to become the 'Cornish Riviera Express'. Along with the 'Flying Dutchman', which ran from London to Exeter in 1849, the Paddington to Birkenhead 'Zulu' of 1880 and the 'Cornishman' of 1890, the 'Cornish Riviera' must rank among the most famous G.W.R. express trains. It certainly played its part in the company's attempts to develop Cornwall as a winter holiday resort, and in order to attract passengers' attention to the possibilities of Cornwall, fresh flowers from the Duchy were displayed at Paddington station throughout the winter months.

The carriages of the Great Western had always been of a reasonably advanced

24 The beginning of the idea of the 'Cornish Riviera'.

design. From the beginning the company was ahead of its contemporaries in building 6-wheeled carriages instead of the then usual 4-wheeled design, and this remained standard practice until the introduction of the standard gauge 8-wheelers in 1874. Some of the early coaches were built to the full width of $10\frac{1}{2}$ ft. permitted by the broad gauge, and seated first-class passengers four a side, but later many G.W. coaches appeared with standard gauge bodies on broad gauge bogies, and so were ready for the conversion of the gauge.

Towards the end of the nineteenth century, the G.W.R. made two notable contributions to the design of rolling-stock. In 1881, William Dean, locomotive superintendent, produced an advanced sleeping-car in which the beds were arranged across the coach and placed two by two in separate compartments. This arrangement proved itself much more acceptable to the travelling public than the undivided sleeping carriages used on the northern lines, and in fact was the forerunner of the modern sleeping coach.

Ten years later, again thanks to Dean, the G.W.R. introduced into this country the first all-corridor train, but the guard only had access throughout, to ensure that second- and third-class passengers could not disturb their first-class fellows! The Great Western had, however, by this time outgrown its positive dislike of third-class passengers seen originally in the windowless, unlit carriages it had provided for them in the 1840s, and by the beginning of the twentieth century, the principal trains of the Great Western offered reasonable accommodation for all.

25 The first British 'Pacific' was Churchward's *Great Bear* of 1908.

Like many other railway companies, the G.W.R. had bought its early locomotives from outside engineering firms, but Daniel Gooch, locomotive superintendent from 1837, was never very happy with their design and by January 1843 he was opening the Great Western's own locomotive shop at Swindon. The first engine built there in 1847 was an enlarged version of the 2-2-2 'Firefly' class and appropriately named the *Great Western*.

In 1854 additional locomotive shops were built at Stafford Road, Wolverhampton, where Joseph Armstrong was appointed to supervise the construction of narrow gauge engines. Ten years later when he succeeded Daniel Gooch as superintendent at Swindon, he continued to produce the 2-2-2 express passenger engines; 60 being built at Swindon between the years 1866 and 1879.

Perhaps the most graceful of the G.W.R. engines were the 7 ft. 8 in. singles designed by Dean and for some years they handled most of the non-stop running on the G.W.R. main lines. By 1898, however, sterner and more functional Dean locomotives were being produced in the 'Bulldog' and 'Atbara' 4-4-0s, and these were followed in 1903 by Churchward's famous 4-4-0 'City' class engines.

The last locomotives built for the broad gauge were designed to be convertible for use on standard gauge tracks by the simple expedient of putting the wheels, originally outside, inside the main frames. This was a factor in the perpetuation, on the Great Western, of a decidedly nineteenth-century style of locomotive long after it had ceased to be built for other companies. And yet G. J. Churchward, who became locomotive superintendent in 1902, was at the same time preparing to equip the railway with a stock of standard locomotives which were unquestionably the most modern and efficient in Great Britain, and remained unsurpassed, for their size, during the rest of the steam era.

The distinguishing marks of the first Churchward standard locomotives were an austerity of appearance wholly alien to the British tradition, and a tapered boiler barrel joined to an oppositely tapered square-topped firebox. The inspiration of these designs was American, but the perfection of their details was very much in the Swindon tradition. Another foreign influence appeared with the importation of three French four-cylinder compounds, of superb but intricate design, many features of which were adopted by Churchward, and which led in particular to the four-cylinder express locomotives used for the most important duties. These engines, the 'Stars', were the models for the post-grouping 'Castles' and 'Kings' of C. B. Collett.

At the grouping in 1923, the Great Western acquired a large number of locomotives from the smaller railway companies merged with it, and of these, very many were excellent machines built for the South Wales coal traffic. Eventually they all passed through Swindon works to emerge with the unmistakable Great Western look, conferred sometimes by details, sometimes by more fundamental changes such as tapered boilers. This was symbolic : so strong was the personality of the old company that it completely transformed its new partners, and the livery of the locomotives and carriages, the painting of the stations, and the perpetuation of the old coat of arms—London and Bristol side by side—all served to proclaim the emergence of the Greater Western Railway.

MAJOR ROUTES OF THE MIDLAND RAILWAY inc. LONDON, TILBURY & SOUTHEND

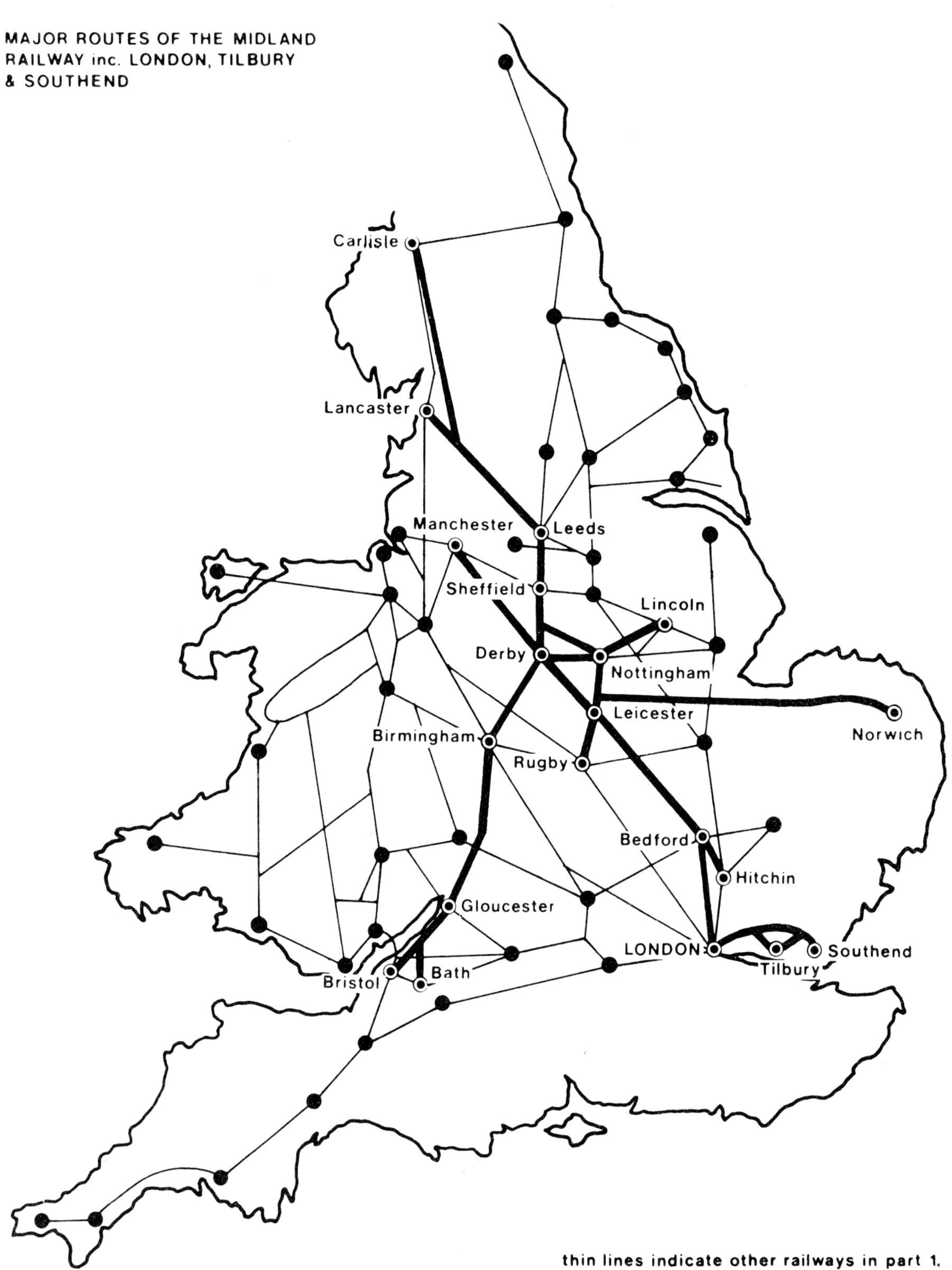

thin lines indicate other railways in part 1.

The Midland Railway

When the London, Midland and Scottish Railway came into existence on 1 January 1923, by far the largest of its constituents was the L.N.W.R. In spite of the status and undoubted efficiency of the 'Premier Line', it was, however, the ideas and men of the Midland Railway that gained ascendancy in the new group. And the Midland was a very different concern from the L.N.W.R. in almost every way in which two large railway companies can differ, while still existing in the same country and serving many of the same areas.

It is perhaps a remarkable indication of the advantages of the pre-grouping railway scene that the two railways could be so different, and it was one of the disadvantages of the grouping that one of these two had to achieve some sort of supremacy over the other. There is no doubt that in 1923 the L.N.W.R. was in a politically weak position, having rested on its great traditions perhaps a little too long, having lost the services of many of its most experienced officers, and being in the middle of a motive power crisis caused largely by the Great War. The Midland had fared better. Its pioneering of centralised train control, helped by the lesser complexity of its system, had enabled it to present an image of greater efficiency. It had officers who were experienced yet comparatively young, and its small

26 One of Matthew Kirtley's long-lived goods engines, fitted in later years with a Johnson cab. Some of these lasted into the period of nationalisation, being then about eighty years old.

27 St. Pancras Station, when first opened in 1868.

locomotives were well maintained and not overworked. The takeover of the London, Tilbury and Southend Railway in 1912 was evidence of an enterprising management.

Originally the Midland had been a collection of lines in the Midlands, but circumstances had obliged it to make a late arrival in the capital—St. Pancras was opened in 1868—and similarly to provide itself with its own route to Scotland, across the Pennines to Carlisle. It had one secondary main line from the Midlands to Bristol, on which was located the steepest main line gradient, of any great length, in Britain—between Lickey and Bromsgrove, at an inclination of 1 in 37. This was, and is, one of the most interesting pieces of line in the country, and for long provided an unusual spectacle of some sort. In the very early days special locomotives were imported from Norris of Philadelphia for this gradient—a remarkable event at a time when British engineers were building many of Europe's first railway routes. In the heyday of the Midland, goods trains were helped up the bank by as many as four extra engines pushing at the rear, and in the last years of steam, British Railways sent there the largest and most powerful steam locomotive ever to run in Britain, the six-cylinder Garratt built in 1925 for the L.N.E.R.

Midland policy was never to run trains of excessive weight. This applied equally to goods and passenger services, and was compensated by greater frequency. Consequently the locomotives were never very large. From the point of view of the passenger, there was a great deal to be said for a frequent service of light and reasonably speedy trains to all destinations. To add to this attraction, the Midland provided extremely good carriages, was quick to provide third-class accommodation on all trains, and was the first to abolish second-class altogether, claiming to provide this style of comfort for its third-class passengers.

If the Midland lacked the grandeur of the North Western, it nevertheless had style. St. Pancras station, inside, was an elegant place: its large and well formed single-span roof vaulted over the platforms in a way which produced the effect of an interior—an interior well furnished with handsome trains. Most of the carriages had clerestories upon their roofs, the older ones square cut, and the newer ones more rounded. Their colour was crimson lake, and the locomotives wore the same livery.

Before 1912, St. Pancras might well contain a train of the London, Tilbury and Southend Railway, which had come round a loop line, off the Tilbury main line, through north east London. This train would be of varnished teak carriages, and its locomotive a very bright green, picked out with brown and vermilion edges, and panelled with black and white lines. This bright stranger would also have a name in gold. The Midland engines were no less handsome, but relatively unadorned, and when the Midland took over the L.T.S.R. uniformity reigned beneath St. Pancras' roof.

The L.T.S.R. was a remarkable small railway, with a main line which ran from east London to Shoeburyness, rather over 40 miles. Most of its trains started from the Great Eastern terminus at Fenchurch Street and its fast commuter services ran to Southend and beyond, via Upminster. Between Barking and Pitsea there was an older but equally important route through Tilbury, and the jointly-owned tracks from St. Pancras ran through Tottenham on their way to Barking, providing

29 The interior of a Pullman Drawing Room car.

important links with the Great Eastern main lines. Over all this system the L.T.S.R. ran an extensive traffic, which included boat expresses for Tilbury, business expresses for Southend, and a large goods traffic serving the area and much of dockland.

Technically, this small railway was very advanced. Its locomotives were mostly 4-4-2 tank engines with outside cylinders, to a design first produced by William Adams for the L.T.S.R. in 1880, and perpetuated in an enlarged version by the L.M.S. as late as 1930. In 1912, just at the time of the Midland takeover, the L.T.S.R. produced the first—and handsomest—British 4-6-4T. It was the second railway to have all its carriages electrically lit, and as a result of close working arrangements with the District Railway, its inner suburban services were operated electrically as part of the underground system, in spite of which it contributed 94 steam locomotives to the Midland stock. Geographically, the natural links of the railway were with the Great Eastern, but the Midland was better placed to make a tempting offer for this prosperous concern, and having acquired it, made few changes—and this went for the L.M.S. as well.

Midland locomotive history was dominated by a remarkable man named Matthew Kirtley, who ruled over the locomotive department for the first thirty years of the Midland's existence. When the railways were nationalised, Kirtley goods engines, around eighty years old, were still doing useful work. Kirtley was scarcely an innovator, but he took as a prototype the Stephenson six-wheeled 'Patent' locomotive of the 1830s and steadily enlarged it and improved the details of design and material without once departing from its basic concept of an inside-cylinder, double-framed, six-wheeled engine with a deep firebox between the middle (cranked) and trailing axles. Only his last few 2-4-0 express engines had single framing for the coupled wheels. His standard wheel spacing became sacrosanct, not only on the Midland, but even on the L.M.S. where it was applied to W. A. Stanier's 2-6-4 tanks and even to the Garratt goods engines, where none of the original considerations which had influenced Kirtley could have any possible relevance.

Kirtley's greatest claim to fame in the wider history of locomotive engineering lies in the fact that it was under his guidance that the best solution was found to the problem of burning coal properly in a locomotive firebox. Before this, coke was the usual fuel on all lines. This innovation, together with his dogged persistence in the unspectacular process of perfecting details, shows Kirtley to have been exactly the type of engineer needed by the railways in the middle of the nineteenth century.

Samuel Waite Johnson, who followed Kirtley, is best remembered as a locomotive artist. Midland policy dictating more, rather than heavier, trains, Johnson was not called upon for innovations until quite late in his career. Much of his energy seems to have been devoted to delineating the perfect shape for a chimney, or even some quite inconspicuous detail. The basic form of Midland engines was already good, and Johnson made them lovely, and rather frail looking. However, the luxurious carriages also dictated by Midland policy eventually called for something a great deal sturdier, and at this stage Johnson profited by his friendship with Walter Smith and Wilson Worsdell of the North Eastern, to the extent of building an enlarged version of Smith's celebrated three-cylinder compound, no. 1619 of the

30 S. W. Johnson's beautiful single-driver locomotives had short lives as trains became heavier, but one is preserved.

N.E.R. The first Midland compound, in a slightly altered form, is preserved in the York Railway Museum, still in excellent working order. It was the forerunner of a class of 45 on the Midland, increased by another 195 by the L.M.S., and there were no better engines, for their weight, on British railways than this class of economical and smooth-running engines which were part of the railway scene for over half a century.

Johnson was succeeded by R. M. Deeley, and Deeley by Sir Henry Fowler, who became the second chief mechanical engineer of the L.M.S., but the only real event in later Midland locomotive history was the building of the Lickey 'banker'—the four-cylinder ten-coupled monster which was the only big engine the Midland ever ran, and which spent most of forty years on one short stretch of track.

At the end of its separate existence, the Midland had enough vitality and individual character to dominate the largest of the four group railways. How the system had grown from its modest beginnings to such a position of influence must now be recounted.

The Midland Railway Company was formed on 10 May 1844, largely through the efforts of George Hudson, railway tycoon and three times Lord Mayor of York. As it was Hudson's vision which had earlier secured through railway communication for the city of York, so now in 1844, it was Hudson's vision which shaped the future for three struggling railway companies in the Midlands, the Birmingham and Derby Junction, opened in 1839, the Midland Counties, opened in 1840, and the North Midland, also opened in 1840.

The Midland Counties, with its metals running from Derby to Nottingham and through Leicester, to join the London and Birmingham line near Rugby, had from its opening engaged in keen, cut-price competition with the Birmingham and Derby Junction Railway, for traffic to and from Derby. The competition had proved ruinous for both parties. The North Midland on the other hand, with its line from Derby via Chesterfield and Rotherham to Leeds, while enjoying a virtual monopoly in its area, was nonetheless in debt from heavy working expenses and over-ambitious expansion. It was in these circumstances that George Hudson, as one of the North Midland directors, took the initiative in suggesting the amalgamation of the three companies as the most positive step towards prosperity. Almost as a matter of course Hudson was then elected chairman of the new Midland Railway so formed.

The company at this date had no independent line into London, but Hudson on assuming his duties as chairman had not neglected to endorse the friendly relations already existing between the Midland Counties and the Birmingham and Derby Junction Railways on the one hand, and the London and Birmingham Railway on the other, so ensuring Midland access to the capital. The most urgent problem then facing Hudson was the challenge of the proposed Great Northern line which threatened to undercut his own London to York rail services via Rugby, Leicester, Derby and Normanton. To counter this opposition Hudson employed all means open to him. On the one hand he instigated investigations into the finance of the proposed G.N., in search of weaknesses sufficient for the rejection of the plans; on the other he put forward schemes for extending the Midland lines to serve the major cities and towns which would be served by the G.N. line. The Midland eastward expansion of 1846–8, with two new lines being laid from Nottingham through Newark to Lincoln, and from Syston, near Leicester, to Peterborough, took place largely as a result of this policy. The G.N., however, in spite of all obstructions, obtained its Act of Parliament authorising the construction of its line in 1846. George Hudson and the Midland Railway had sustained a defeat.

Nevertheless, during the same year 1846, there was success for the young company on another front, with the absorption of three hitherto independent lines; the Leicester and Swannington Railway, opened in 1933 to carry coal to Leicester, the Birmingham and Gloucester Railway, opened in 1840, and the Bristol and Gloucester Railway, opened in 1844.

Then came Hudson's proposal for the Midland to purchase the Leeds and Bradford line; a proposal which highlighted Hudson's many conflicting interests, for in this case, much to the chagrin of the Midland board, he was revealed as both buyer and seller. The Midland did acquire the Leeds and Bradford, but not until 1851, that is two years after Hudson had been forced to resign as chairman of the Midland company, because of the shareholders' increasing lack of confidence in him.

John Ellis, the deputy chairman and a very able administrator, then stepped into the vacant position. It was during Ellis's term of office that the Midland acquired its second entrance to London, this time over Great Northern metals. The volume of goods traffic travelling to London, via the Midland and L.N.W. lines, had increased enormously since about 1848, with the result that serious delays for the Midland wagons on the London and North Western line from Rugby were all too common.

In 1853 therefore an Act of Parliament was obtained for an extension of Midland metals from Leicester to join the Great Northern at Hitchin. The extension was completed and opened in 1857, but as the volume of traffic flowing south on the Midland line continued to increase, the new route, even in the short term, failed to solve the congestion and delay. Unfortunately, the Great Northern track from Hitchin to King's Cross consisted of one up and one down line only, and quite naturally the Great Northern, in spite of levying heavy tolls on the Midland trains using its track, always gave priority to its own traffic.

Such a situation could not be viewed as satisfactory by the Midland Railway and

31 Midland Railway first- and third-class twelve-wheeled bogie coach with luggage compartment. Such luxury was unusual in 1876.

therefore in October 1862, four years after the accession of the chairman, William Price, the Midland board passed a resolution to build its own independent line to a London terminus at St. Pancras. The 50-mile line, from Bedford through Luton and St. Albans, was completed and opened for goods traffic towards the end of 1867. Passenger traffic was allowed on the line in the following year when the St. Pancras passenger station was almost completed. (In fact men were still at work on the booking hall and other offices, when the first passenger trains arrived.) This extension of the Midland main line into London was a very important step in the history of the Midland railway, for it thrust the company into the thick of the competition for northern and Scottish traffic.

Direct independent access to Scotland was also seen as one of the pressing needs of the Midland company if it was to compete in earnest with the East and West Coast services. As early as 1852 the Midland had obtained a lease on the 'Little North Western' Railway, which had given it a line from Skipton to Morecambe with a branch to Ingleton. It was this branch line which offered possibilities of northward expansion for the Midland, but nothing was then done, and in 1861 the L.N.W. also seeing the possibilities had built its own line from Carlisle, to form a head-on junction with the Midland (at Ingleton) and so keep the company within reasonable bounds.

Then in 1866 came a new Midland plan, authorised by Act of Parliament, for a line leaving the Little North Western at Settle and running, through some extremely difficult terrain, to Carlisle. It was not until 1869, when finance permitted, that work on this new line was begun and then so arduous proved the task of laying the track through the hills that the extension was not finally completed until 1876, three years behind schedule. Once opened it did enable the Midland to develop its own London-Scottish traffic independently of its neighbours and rivals. Four Midland Scottish express trains, two up and two down, ran on the new Carlisle extension in 1876, two travelling to and from Glasgow, by courtesy of the Glasgow and South Western company, and two travelling to and from Edinburgh by courtesy of the North British Company.

To attract passengers from parallel rival services to the north and to Scotland, the

Midland adopted some revolutionary proposals concerning fares and comfort on its passenger trains, for which it is rightly remembered. In 1872, largely on the suggestion of the then general manager, James Allport, the Midland railway had announced that henceforth all its trains would carry third-class passengers. The decision was bold and enlightened, the response overwhelming. By 1875, 83½% of passengers travelling on the Midland railway were third-class passengers. So came the next major reorganisation in this direction, again under the guidance of James Allport, now joined by a new chairman, Edward Shipley Ellis, son of John. The new proposal was for the complete abolition of second-class travel and the reduction of first-class fares to the previous second-class level. The decision to adopt this scheme, taken in 1874, was not fully implemented until 1875, but again the response from the travelling public was, as expected, enthusiastic, and eventually other companies were forced to follow the Midland lead.

It was with an eye to the comfort of passengers travelling on Midland trains, that Mr. Allport introduced the American Pullman cars into this country early in 1874. By June 1874 these cars, which were to have such an influence on the development of English bogie stock, were in regular service on the Midland Bradford–St. Pancras route. By 1875 Pullman sleeping-cars were in use on the London–Liverpool line and the following year they were brought into service on the new Midland Scottish route. During the 1880s and 90s, the company did not involve itself in the famous East and West Coast races to Scotland, but it did continue its policy of improving passenger facilities and lowering passenger fares wherever possible. As a result, during these two decades, it reduced the supplementary fares on Pullman sleeping-cars from 7/- to 5/-, it expanded its dining facilities and in 1892 it produced the 60-ft. Midland dining-car, with a smoking lounge, a main dining room, a pantry and a kitchen. By 1899 the carriage and wagon department at Derby, the company's headquarters, was overwhelmed with the amount of work it was being called upon to perform, mainly for the London–Scottish services.

In earlier years, ensuring the punctuality of its passenger trains tended to be a problem with the Midland, one reason for this being the volume of the company's goods traffic flowing from Liverpool, from Manchester, from the West Riding and from other centres, which frequently cluttered the main lines, especially around Derby and Leicester, causing innumerable delays. It was to alleviate this congestion that secondary lines were constructed, in 1875 from Ambergate to Clay Cross, and from Trowell to Radford, just north of Nottingham; in 1879 from Nottingham to Melton Mowbray and then on to rejoin the main line at Kettering. The goods traffic could therefore be diverted from Derby and Leicester, and away from the main passenger route between Ambergate and Kettering. The congestion problem was never completely solved, however, and in 1907, the Midland created a specific post of General Superintendent for the supervision of traffic flow on the main lines, and became the pioneer of centralised train control.

Throughout its independent existence the Midland railway never ceased to expand. In 1867, a line from Derby to New Mills had been constructed, giving the Midland access to Manchester over Manchester, Sheffield and Lincolnshire metals, and in 1902 the company extended the line to form its own entrance to Manchester

Central. In 1903 the Midland acquired the Belfast and Northern Counties Railway, which in itself was a stimulus for the company to develop the port of Heysham, and in 1904 to begin steamer services to Ireland. In 1906 the company acquired a half share in the County Donegal lines, and in 1912 came the Midland's final, somewhat surprising, acquisition of the London, Tilbury and Southend Railway.

On the eve of the grouping, the Midland was remembered for many things. It was remembered for its enlightened passenger carrying policies which brought cheap travel for the many; it was remembered for the cleanliness and the finish of its rolling-stock, its crimson carriages lined with yellow being given anything up to four or five coats of varnish and innumerable preparatory coats of gold size, turpentine and filling; and it was remembered for the outstanding personnel, Hudson, Allport, Ellis, Kirtley, Johnson and others who had helped to turn the Midland from a provincial system into a trunk railway joining London and Bristol to the Scottish border. Within the L.M.S. group, the character of the Midland was to survive the next twenty-five years surprisingly unchanged, as more and more small locomotives of Midland type came from Crewe as well as Derby, and the Midland crimson came to adorn the luxurious new products of Wolverton carriage works as well.

With nationalisation, the Midland colour disappeared from the locomotives, but it soon became universal on all British passenger stock, and it was only when steam traction came to an end, the last of the innumerable Midland locomotive types went to the scrap heap, and the new 'rail blue' livery appeared on the carriages, that the memory of the Midland faded from the tracks of British Railways. But in many stations, grandiose or picturesque, the memory is still strongly awakened.

32 The frail and beautiful Johnson look in a 4-4-0 express engine of the 'nineties.

G.N.R.
SKEGNESS
IS SO BRACING

Printed in the UK for HMSO
Dd 736271 C40 12/83